Start Where You Are

A GUIDE TO COMPASSIONATE LIVING

PEMA CHÖDRÖN

SHAMBHALA
Boston
2004

FRONTISPIECE: Gampo Abbey, Cape Breton, Nova Scotia.
Photograph by Liza Matthews

SHAMBHALA PUBLICATIONS, INC.
Horticultural Hall
300 Massachusetts Avenue
Boston, Massachusetts 02115
www.shambhala.com

© 1994 by Pema Chödrön

Translation of *The Root Text of the Seven Points of Training the Mind*
© 1981, 1986 by Chögyam Trungpa; revised translation © 1993 by
Diana J. Mukpo and the Nālandā Translation Committee. *The
Sādhana of Māhamudrā* © 1968, 1976 by Chögyam Trungpa.

*The author's proceeds from this book will be donated to Gampo Abbey,
Pleasant Bay, Nova Scotia, Canada B0E 2P0.*

9 8 7 6 5 4 3 2

PRINTED IN CHINA
♾ This edition is printed on acid-free paper that meets the
American National Standards Institute z39.48 Standard.
Distributed in the United States by Random House, Inc.,
and in Canada by Random House of Canada Ltd

The Library of Congress catalogues the previous edition of this title as follows:
Chödrön, Pema.
Start where you are: a guide to compassionate living/Pema Chödrön.—1st ed.
p. cm.
Includes bibliographical references.
ISBN 978-0-87773-880-0 (alk. paper)
ISBN 978-1-57062-839-9 (pbk.)
ISBN 978-1-59030-142-5 (Shambhala Library)
1. Spiritual life—Buddhism. 2. Buddhism—China—Tibet—Doctrines.
I. Title.
BQ7805.C49 1994   93-39135
294.3'444—dc20   CIP

To my mother, Virginia, and
my granddaughter, Alexandria

CONTENTS

PREFACE

T HIS BOOK is about awakening the heart. If you
have ever wondered how to awaken your genuine compassionate heart, this book will serve as
a guide.

   In our era, when so many people are seeking help
to relate to their own feelings of woundedness and
at the same time wanting to help relieve the suffering they see around them, the ancient teachings
presented here are especially encouraging and to
the point. When we find that we are closing down to
ourselves and to others, here is instruction on how
to open. When we find that we are holding back,
here is instruction on how to give. That which is unwanted and rejected in ourselves and in others can
be seen and felt with honesty and compassion. This
is teaching on how to be there for others without
withdrawing.

   I first encountered these teachings in *The Great
Path of Awakening* by the nineteenth-century Tibetan
teacher Jamgön Kongtrül the Great. Called the *lojong* teachings, they include a very supportive meditation practice called *tonglen* and the practice of
working with the seven points of mind training,

which comes from an old Tibetan text called *The Root Text of the Seven Points of Training the Mind,* by Chekawa Yeshe Dorje. (See appendix.)

Lojong means "mind training." The lojong teachings are organized around seven points that contain fifty-nine pithy slogans that remind us how to awaken our hearts.* Working with the slogans constitutes the heart of this book. These teachings belong to the mahayana school of Buddhism, which emphasizes compassionate communication and compassionate relationship with others. They also emphasize that we are not as solid as we think. In truth, there is enormous space in which to live our everyday lives. They help us see that the sense of a separate, isolated self and a separate, isolated other is a painful misunderstanding that we could see through and let go.

Tonglen means "taking in and sending out." This meditation practice is designed to help ordinary people like ourselves connect with the openness and softness of our hearts. Instead of shielding and protecting our soft spot, with tonglen we could let ourselves feel what it is to be human. By so doing, we could widen our circle of compassion. Through this book I hope others may find such encouragement.

When I first read the lojong teachings I was struck by their unusual message that we can use our difficulties and problems to awaken our hearts. Rather

---

*The slogans are also available as a set of cards that one could use as an aid in working with these teachings. See page 217 for information.

than seeing the unwanted aspects of life as obstacles, Jamgön Kongtrül presented them as the raw material necessary for awakening genuine uncontrived compassion: we can start where we are. Whereas in Kongtrül's commentary the emphasis is primarily on taking on the suffering of others, it is apparent that in this present age it is necessary to also emphasize that the first step is to develop compassion for our own wounds. This book stresses repeatedly that it is unconditional compassion for ourselves that leads naturally to unconditional compassion for others. If we are willing to stand fully in our own shoes and never give up on ourselves, then we will be able to put ourselves in the shoes of others and never give up on them. True compassion does not come from wanting to help out those less fortunate than ourselves but from realizing our kinship with all beings.

Later I heard these instructions presented in a more contemporary mode by my own teacher, Chögyam Trungpa, Rinpoche. (These have now been published in the book *Training the Mind and Cultivating Loving-Kindness.*) Trungpa Rinpoche pointed out that he had first been given these teachings when he was quite young and that it was a great relief to him to find that Buddhism could be so practical and so helpful in everyday life. He was inspired to find that we could bring everything we encounter to the path and use it to awaken our intelligence, our compassion, and our ability to take a fresh look.

In the winters of 1992 and 1993, I led one-month practice periods, called *dathuns,* completely dedicated to these lojong teachings and to the meditation practice of tonglen. Most important, those of us participating wanted to put these instructions into practice continually as the inevitable frustrations and difficulties of daily life arose. We saw the dathun as a chance to take the instructions to heart and apply them in all situations, especially those in which we usually prefer to blame or criticize or ignore. That is, we saw it as a chance to use the teachings to relate on the spot with an open heart and an open mind to the aggression, the craving, and the denial that we find in ourselves and in others.

Even for those who are unfamiliar with meditation, the lojong teachings present the possibility of an entire change of attitude: we could relate compassionately with that which we prefer to push away, and we could learn to give away and share that which we hold most dear.

For those who feel prepared to practice sitting meditation and tonglen meditation and to work with the lojong slogans in an ongoing way, doing so may be the beginning of learning what it really means to love. This is a method for allowing a lot of space, so that people can relax and open. This is the path of unconditional compassionate living. It is designed especially for people who find themselves living in times of darkness. May it be of benefit.

ACKNOWLEDGMENTS

I WOULD LIKE to acknowledge the help of Pat Cousineau and Lynne Vande Bunte, who did most of the typing, and of Judith Anderson, Marilyn Hayes, Trime Lhamo, Lynne Vande Bunte, and Helen Tashima, who did the transcribing. Also thanks to Pam Gaines, who not only typed but also found people to help, and especially to Migme Chödrön, who did the first edit of the original manuscript and was a constant support to me during all the steps of preparing this book. Last but certainly not least, I want to thank Emily Hilburn Sell of Shambhala Publications. I feel extremely fortunate that she once again agreed to transform the talks into their final form.

Start Where You Are

I

No Escape, No Problem

WE ALREADY HAVE everything we need. There is no need for self-improvement. All these trips that we lay on ourselves—the heavy-duty fearing that we're bad and hoping that we're good, the identities that we so dearly cling to, the rage, the jealousy and the addictions of all kinds—never touch our basic wealth. They are like clouds that temporarily block the sun. But all the time our warmth and brilliance are right here. This is who we really are. We are one blink of an eye away from being fully awake.

Looking at ourselves this way is very different from our usual habit. From this perspective we don't need to change: you can feel as wretched as you like, and you're still a good candidate for enlightenment. You can feel like the world's most hopeless basket case, but that feeling is your wealth, not something to be thrown out or improved upon. There's a richness to all of the smelly stuff that we so dislike and so little desire. The delightful things—what we love so dearly about ourselves, the places in which we feel some sense of pride or inspiration—these also are our wealth.

With the practices presented in this book, you can start just where you are. If you're feeling angry, poverty-stricken, or depressed, the practices described here were designed for you, because they will encourage you to use all the unwanted things in your life as the means for awakening compassion for yourself and others. These practices show us how to accept ourselves, how to relate directly with suffering, how to stop running away from the painful aspects of our lives. They show us how to work openheartedly with life just as it is.

When we hear about compassion, it naturally brings up working with others, caring for others. The reason we're often not there for others—whether for our child or our mother or someone who is insulting us or someone who frightens us—is that we're not there for ourselves. There are whole parts of ourselves that are so unwanted that whenever they begin to come up we run away.

Because we escape, we keep missing being right here, being right on the dot. We keep missing the moment we're in. Yet if we can experience the moment we're in, we discover that it is unique, precious, and completely fresh. It never happens twice. One can appreciate and celebrate each moment—there's nothing more sacred. There's nothing more vast or absolute. In fact, there's nothing more!

Only to the degree that we've gotten to know our personal pain, only to the degree that we've related with pain at all, will we be fearless enough, brave enough, and enough of a warrior to be willing to feel the pain of others. To that degree we will be able to take on the pain of others because we will have discovered that their pain and our own pain are not different.

However, to do this, we need all the help we can get. It is my hope that this book will supply that help. The tools you will be given are three very supportive practices:

1. Basic sitting meditation (called *shamatha-vipashyana* meditation)
2. The practice of taking in and sending out (called tonglen)
3. The practice of working with slogans (called the seven points of mind training, or lojong)

All these practices awaken our trust that the wisdom and compassion that we need are already within us. They help us to know ourselves: our rough parts and our smooth parts, our passion, aggression, ignorance, and wisdom. The reason that people harm other people, the reason that the planet is polluted and people and animals are not doing so well these days is that individuals don't know or trust or love themselves enough. The technique of sitting called shamatha-vipashyana ("tranquillity-insight") is like a golden key that helps us to know ourselves.

Shamatha-Vipashyana Meditation

In shamatha-vipashyana meditation, we sit upright with legs crossed and eyes open, hands resting on our thighs. Then we simply become aware of our breath as it goes out. It requires precision to be right there with that breath. On the other hand, it's extremely relaxed and extremely soft. Saying, "Be right there with the breath as it goes out," is the same thing as saying, "Be fully present." Be right here with whatever is going on. Being aware of the breath as it goes out, we may also be aware of other things going on—sounds on the street, the light on the walls. These things may capture our attention slightly, but they don't need to draw us off. We can continue to sit right here, aware of the breath going out.

But being with the breath is only part of the technique. These thoughts that run through our minds continually are the other part. We sit here talking to ourselves. The instruction is that when you realize you've been thinking, you label it "thinking." When your mind wanders off, you say to yourself, "Thinking." Whether your thoughts are violent or passionate or full of ignorance and denial; whether your thoughts are worried or fearful, whether your thoughts are spiritual thoughts, pleasing thoughts of how well you're doing, comforting thoughts, uplifting thoughts, whatever they are, without judgment or harshness simply label it all "thinking," and do that with honesty and gentleness.

The touch on the breath is light: only about 25 percent of the awareness is on the breath. You're not grasping or fixating on it. You're opening, letting the breath mix with the space of the room, letting your breath just go out into space. Then there's something like a pause, a gap until the next breath goes out again. While you're breathing in, there could be some sense of just opening and waiting. It is like pushing the doorbell and waiting for someone to answer. Then you push the doorbell again and wait for someone to answer. Then probably your mind wanders off and you realize you're thinking again—at this point, use the labeling technique.

It's important to be faithful to the technique. If you find that your labeling has a harsh, negative tone to it, as if you were saying, "Dammit!," that you're giving yourself a hard time, say it again and lighten up. It's not like trying to down the thoughts as if they were clay pigeons. Instead, be gentle. Use the labeling part of the technique as an opportunity to develop softness and compassion for yourself. Anything that comes up is okay in the arena of meditation. The point is, you can see it honestly and make friends with it.

Although it is embarrassing and painful, it is very healing to stop hiding from yourself. It is healing to know all the ways that you're sneaky, all tæhe ways that you hide out, all the ways that you shut down, deny, close off, criticize people, all your weird little ways. You can know all that with some sense of humor and kindness. By knowing yourself, you're coming to know humanness altogether. We are all up against these things. We are all in this together. So when you realize that you're talking to yourself, label it "thinking" and notice your tone of voice. Let it be compassionate and gentle and humorous. Then you'll be changing old stuck patterns that are shared by the whole human race. Compassion for others begins with kindness to ourselves.*

Lojong Practice

The heart of this book is the lojong practice and teachings. The lojong practice (or mind training) has two elements: the practice, which is tonglen meditation, and the teaching, which comes in the form of slogans.

The basic notion of lojong is that we can make friends with what we reject, what we see as "bad" in ourselves and in other people. At the same time, we could learn to be generous with what we cherish, what we see as "good." If we begin to live in this

---

*If you've never tried sitting meditation before, you may wish to seek the guidance of a qualified meditation instructor. See the list of meditation centers at the back of the book for help in finding an instructor.

way, something in us that may have been buried for a long time begins to ripen. Traditionally this "something" is called *bodhichitta,* or awakened heart. It's something that we already have but usually have not yet discovered.

It's as if we were poor, homeless, hungry, and cold, and although we didn't know it, right under the ground where we always slept was a pot of gold. That gold is like bodhichitta. Our confusion and misery come from not knowing that the gold is right here and from always looking for it somewhere else. When we talk about joy, enlightenment, waking up, or awakening bodhichitta, all that means is that we know the gold is right here, and we realize that it's been here all along.

The basic message of the lojong teachings is that if it's painful, you can learn to hold your seat and move closer to that pain. Reverse the usual pattern, which is to split, to escape. Go against the grain and hold your seat. Lojong introduces a different attitude toward unwanted stuff: if it's painful, you become willing not just to endure it but also to let it awaken your heart and soften you. You learn to embrace it.

If an experience is delightful or pleasant, usually we want to grab it and make it last. We're afraid that it will end. We're not inclined to share it. The lojong teachings encourage us, if we enjoy what we are experiencing, to think of other people and wish for them to feel that. Share the wealth. Be generous with your joy. Give away what you most want. Be generous with your insights and delights. Instead of fearing that they're going to slip away and holding on to them, share them.

Whether it's pain or pleasure, through lojong practice we come to have a sense of letting our experience be as it is without trying to manipulate it, push it away, or grasp it. The pleasurable aspects of being human as well as the painful ones become the key to awakening bodhichitta.

There is a saying that is the underlying principle of tonglen and slogan practice: "Gain and victory to others, loss and defeat to myself." The Tibetan word for pride or arrogance, which is *nga-gyal,* is literally in English "me-victorious." Me first. Ego. That kind of "me-victorious" attitude is the cause of all suffering.

In essence what this little saying is getting at is that words like *victory* and *defeat* are completely interwoven with how we protect ourselves, how we guard our hearts. Our sense of victory just means that we guarded our heart enough so that nothing got through, and we think we won the war. The armor around our soft spot—our wounded heart—is now more fortified, and our world is smaller. Maybe nothing is getting in to scare us for one whole week, but our courage is weakening, and our sense of caring about others is getting completely obscured. Did we really win the war?

On the other hand, our sense of being defeated means that something got in. Something touched our soft spot. This vulnerability that we've kept armored for ages—something touched it. Maybe all that touched it was a butterfly, but we have never been touched there before. It was so tender. Because we have never felt that before, we now go out and buy padlocks and armor and guns so that we will never feel it again. We go for anything—seven pairs of boots that fit inside each other so we don't have to feel the ground, twelve masks so that no one can see our real face, nineteen sets of armor so that nothing can touch our skin, let alone our heart.

These words *defeat* and *victory* are so tied up with how we stay imprisoned. The real confusion is caused by not knowing that we have limitless wealth, and the confusion deepens each time we buy into this win/lose logic: if you touch me, that is defeat, and if I manage to armor myself and not be touched, that's victory.

Realizing our wealth would end our bewilderment and confusion. But the only way to do that is to let things fall apart. And that's the very thing that we dread the most—the ultimate defeat. Yet letting things fall apart would actually let fresh air into this old, stale basement of a heart that we've got.

Saying "Loss and defeat to myself" doesn't mean to become a masochist: "Kick my head in, torture me, and dear God, may I never be happy." What it means is that you can open your heart and your mind and know what defeat feels like.

You feel too short, you have indigestion, you're too fat and too stupid. You say to yourself, "Nobody loves me, I'm always left out. I have no teeth, my hair's getting gray, I have blotchy skin, my nose runs." That all comes under the category of defeat, the defeat of ego. We're always not wanting to be who we are. However, we can never connect with our fundamental wealth as long as we are buying into this advertisement hype that we have to be someone else, that we have to smell different or have to look different.

On the other hand, when you say, "Victory to others," instead of wanting to keep it for yourself, there's the sense of sharing the whole delightful aspect of your life. You did lose some weight. You do like the way you look in the mirror. You suddenly feel like you have a nice voice, or someone falls in love with you or you fall in love with someone else. Or the seasons change and it touches your heart, or you begin to notice the snow in Vermont or the way the trees move in the wind. With anything that you want, you begin to develop the attitude of wanting to share it instead of being stingy with it or fearful around it.

Perhaps the slogans will challenge you. They say things like "Don't be jealous," and you think, "How did they know?" Or "Be grateful to everyone"; you wonder how to do that or why to bother. Some slogans, such as "Always meditate on whatever provokes resentment," exhort you to go beyond common sense. These slogans are not always the sort of thing that you would want to hear, let alone find inspiring, but if we work with them, they will become like our breath, our eyesight, our first thought. They will become like the smells we smell and the sound we hear. We can let them permeate our whole being. That's the point. These slogans aren't theoretical or abstract. They are about exactly who we are and what is happening to us. They are completely relevant to how we experience things, how we relate with whatever occurs in our lives. They are about how to relate with pain and fear and pleasure and joy, and how those things can transform us fully and completely. When we work with the slogans, ordinary life becomes the path of awakening.

2

No Big Deal

THE PRACTICES we'll be doing help us develop trust in our awakened heart, our bodhichitta. If we could finally grasp how rich we are, our sense of heavy burden would diminish, and our sense of curiosity would increase.

Bodhichitta has three qualities: (1) it is soft and gentle, which is compassion; (2) at the same time, it is clear and sharp, which is called *prajna;* and (3) it is open. This last quality of bodhichitta is called *shunyata* and is also known as emptiness. Emptiness sounds cold. However, bodhichitta isn't cold at all, because there's a heart quality—the warmth of compassion—that pervades the space and the clarity. Compassion and openness and clarity are all one thing, and this one thing is called bodhichitta.

Bodhichitta is our heart—our wounded, softened heart. Now, if you look for that soft heart that we guard so carefully—if you decide that you're going to do a scientific exploration under the microscope and try to find that heart—you won't find it. You can look, but all you'll find is some kind of tenderness. There isn't anything that you can cut out and put under the microscope. There isn't anything that you can dissect or grasp. The more you look, the more you find just a feeling of tenderness tinged with some kind of sadness.

This sadness is not about somebody mistreating us. This is inherent sadness, unconditioned sadness. It has part of our birthright, a family heirloom. It's been called the genuine heart of sadness.

Sometimes we emphasize the compassionate aspect of our genuine heart, and this is called the relative part of bodhichitta. Sometimes we emphasize the open, unfindable aspect of our heart, and this is called the absolute, this genuine heart that is just waiting to be discovered.

The first slogan of the seven points of mind training is "First, train in the preliminaries." The preliminaries are the basic meditation practice—beneficial, supportive, warm-hearted, brilliant shamatha-vipashyana practice. When we say, "First, train in the preliminaries," it's not as if we first do shamatha-vipashyana practice and then graduate to something more advanced. Shamatha-vipashyana practice is not only the earth that we stand on, it's also the air we breathe and the heart that beats inside us. Sha-matha-vipashyana practice is the essence of all other practices as well. So when we say, "First, train in the preliminaries," it simply means that without this good base there's nothing to build on. Without it we couldn't understand tonglen practice—which I'll describe later—and we wouldn't have any insight into our mind, into either our craziness or our wisdom.

Next, there are five slogans that emphasize the openness of bodhichitta, the absolute quality of bodhichitta. These point to the fact that, although we are usually very caught up with the solidness and seriousness of life, we could begin to stop making such a big deal and connect with the spacious and joyful aspect of our being.

The first of the absolute slogans is "Regard all dharmas as dreams." More simply, regard everything as a dream. Life is a dream. Death is also a dream, for that matter; waking is a dream and sleeping is a dream. Another way to put this is, "Every situation is a passing memory."

We went for a walk this morning, but now it is a memory. Every situation is a passing memory. As we live our lives, there is a lot of repetition—so many mornings greeted, so many meals eaten, so many drives to work and drives home, so many times spent with our friends and family, again and again, over and over. All of these situations bring up irritation, lust, anger, sadness, all kinds of things about the people with whom we work or live or stand in line or fight traffic. So much will happen in the same way over and over again. It's all an excellent opportunity to connect with this sense of each situation being like a memory.

Just a few moments ago, you were standing in the hall, and now it is a memory. But then it was so real. Now I'm talking, and what I have just said has already passed.

It is said that with these slogans that are pointing to absolute truth—openness—one should not say, "Oh yes, I know," but that one should just allow a mental gap to open, and wonder, "Could it be? Am I dreaming this?" Pinch yourself. Dreams are just as convincing as waking reality. You could begin to contemplate the fact that perhaps things are not as solid or as reliable as they seem.

Sometimes we just have this experience automatically; it happens to us naturally. I read recently about someone who went hiking in the high mountains and was alone in the wilderness at a very high altitude. If any of you have been at high altitudes, you know the light there is different. There's something more blue, more luminous about it. Things seem lighter and not so dense as in the middle of a big city, particularly if you stay there for some time alone. You're sometimes not sure if you're awake or asleep. This man wrote that he began to feel as if he were cooking his meals in a dream and that when he would go for a walk, he was walking toward mountains that were made out of air. He felt that the letter he was writing was made of air, that his hand was a phantom pen writing these phantom words, and that he was going to send it off to a phantom receiver. Sometimes we, too, have that kind of experience, even at sea level. It actually makes our world feel so much bigger.

Without going into this much more, I'd like to bring it down to our shamatha practice. The key is, it's no big deal. We could all just lighten up. Regard all dharmas as dreams. With our minds we make a big deal out of ourselves, out of our pain, and out of our problems.

If someone instructed you to catch the beginning, middle, and end of every thought, you'd find that they don't seem to have a beginning, middle, and end. They definitely are there. You're talking to yourself, you're creating your whole identity, your whole world, your whole sense of problem, your whole sense of contentment, with this continual stream of thought. But if you really try to find thoughts, they're always changing. As the slogan says, each situation and even each word and thought and emotion is passing memory. It's like trying to see when water turns into steam. You can never find that precise moment. You know there's water, because you can drink it and make it into soup and wash in it, and you know there's steam, but you can't see precisely when one changes into the other. Everything is like that.

Have you ever been caught in the heavy-duty scenario of feeling defeated and hurt, and then somehow, for no particular reason, you just drop it? It just goes, and you wonder why you made "much ado about nothing." What was that all about? It also happens when you fall in love with somebody; you're so completely into thinking about the person twenty-four hours a day. You are haunted and you want him or her so badly. Then a little while later, "I don't know where we went wrong, but the feeling's gone and I just can't get it back." We all know this feeling of how we make things a big deal and then realize that we're making a lot out of nothing.

I'd like to encourage us all to lighten up, to practice with a lot of gentleness. This is not the drill sergeant saying, "Lighten up or else." I have found that if we can possibly use anything we hear against ourselves, we usually do. For instance, you find yourself being tense and remember that I said to lighten up, and then you feel, "Basically, I'd better stop sitting because I can't lighten up and I'm not a candidate for discovering bodhichitta or anything else."

Gentleness in our practice and in our life helps to awaken bodhichitta. It's like remembering something. This compassion, this clarity, this openness are like something we have forgotten. Sitting here being gentle with ourselves, we're rediscovering something. It's like a mother reuniting with her child; having been lost to each other for a long, long time, they reunite. The way to reunite with bodhichitta is to lighten up in your practice and in your whole life.

Meditation practice is a formal way in which you can get used to lightening up. I encourage you to follow the instructions faithfully, but within that form to

be extremely gentle. Let the whole thing be soft.
Breathing out, the instruction is to touch your breath
as it goes, to be with your breath. Let that be like relaxing out. Sense the breath going out into big space
and dissolving into space. You're not trying to clutch
it, not trying to furrow your brow and catch that
breath as if you won't be a good person unless you
grab that breath. You're simply relaxing outward with
your breath.

Labeling our thoughts is a powerful support for
lightening up, a very helpful way to reconnect with
shunyata—this open dimension of our being, this
fresh, unbiased dimension of our mind. When we
come to that place where we say, "Thinking," we can
just say it with an unbiased attitude and with tremendous gentleness. Regard the thoughts as bubbles and
the labeling like touching them with a feather.
There's just this light touch—"Thinking"—and they
dissolve back into the space.

Don't worry about achieving. Don't worry about
perfection. Just be there each moment as best you
can. When you realize you've wandered off again,
simply very lightly acknowledge that. This light touch
is the golden key to reuniting with our openness.

The slogan says to regard all dharmas—that is, regard everything—as a dream. In this case, we could
say, "Regard all thoughts as a dream," and just touch
them and let them go. When you notice you're making a really big deal, just notice that with a lot of gen-

tleness, a lot of heart. No big deal. If the thoughts go, and you still feel anxious and tense, you could allow that to be there, with a lot of space around it. Just let it be. When thoughts come up again, see them for what they are. It's no big deal. You can loosen up, lighten up, whatever.

That's the essential meaning of the absolute bodhichitta slogans—to connect with the open, spacious quality of your mind, so that you can see that there's no need to shut down and make such a big deal about everything. Then when you do make a big deal, you can give that a lot of space and let it go.

In sitting practice, there's no way you can go wrong, wherever you find yourself. Just relax. Relax your shoulders, relax your stomach, relax your heart, relax your mind. Bring in as much gentleness as you can. The technique is already quite precise. It has a structure, it has a form. So within that form, move with warmth and gentleness. That's how we awaken bodhichitta.

3
Pulling Out the Rug

As I said before, the main instruction is simply to lighten up. By taking that attitude toward one's practice and one's life, by taking that more gentle and appreciative attitude toward oneself and others, the sense of burden that all of us carry around begins to decrease.

The next slogan is "Examine the nature of unborn awareness." The real intention of this slogan is to pull the rug out from under you in case you think you understood the previous slogan. If you feel proud of yourself because of how you really understood that everything is like a dream, then this slogan is here to challenge that smug certainty. It's saying, "Well, who is this anyway who thinks that they discovered that everything is like a dream?"

"Examine the nature of unborn awareness." Who is this "I"? Where did it come from? Who is the one who realizes anything? Who is it who's aware? This slogan points to the transparency of everything, including our beloved identity, this precious *M-E*. Who is this *me*?

The armor we erect around our soft hearts causes

a lot of misery. But don't be deceived, it's very transparent. The more vivid it gets, the more clearly you see it, the more you realize that this shield—this cocoon—is just made up of thoughts that we churn out and regard as solid. The shield is not made out of iron. The armor is not made out of metal. In fact, it's made out of passing memory.

The absolute quality of bodhichitta can never be pinned down. If you can talk about it, that's not it. So if you think that awakened heart is something, it isn't. It's passing memory. And if you think this big burden of ego, this big monster cocoon, is something, it isn't. It's just passing memory. Yet it's so vivid. The more you practice, the more vivid it gets. It's a paradox—it can't be found, and yet it couldn't be more vivid.

We spend a lot of time trying to nail everything down, concretizing, just trying to make everything solid and secure. We also spend a lot of time trying to dull or soften or fend off that vividness. When we awaken our hearts, we're changing the whole pattern, but not by creating a new pattern. We are moving further and further away from concretizing and making things so solid and always trying to get some ground under our feet. This moving away from comfort and security, this stepping out into what is unknown, uncharted, and shaky—that's called enlightenment, liberation. Krishnamurti talks about it in his book *Liberation from the Known,* Alan Watts in *The Wisdom of Insecurity.* It's all getting at the same thing.

This isn't how we usually go about things, in case you hadn't noticed. We usually try to get ground under our feet. It's as if you were in a spaceship going to the moon, and you looked back at this tiny planet Earth and realized that things were vaster than any mind could conceive and you just couldn't handle it, so you started worrying about what you were going to have for lunch. There you are in outer space with this sense of the world being so vast, and then you bring it all down into this very tiny world of worrying about what's for lunch: hamburgers or hot dogs. We do this all the time.

In "Examine the nature of unborn awareness," *examine* is an interesting word. It's not a matter of looking and seeing—"Now I've got it!"—but a process of examination and contemplation that leads into being able to relax with insecurity or edginess or restlessness. Much joy comes from that.

"Examine the nature of unborn awareness." Simply examine the nature of the one who has insight—contemplate that. We could question this solid identity that we have, this sense of a person frozen in time and space, this monolithic ME. In sitting practice, saying "thinking" with a soft touch introduces a question mark about who is doing all this thinking. Who's churning out what? What's happening to whom? Who am I that's thinking or that's labeling thinking or that's going back to the breath or hurting or wishing lunch would happen soon?

* * *

The next slogan is "Self-liberate even the antidote." In case you think you understood "Examine the nature of unborn awareness," let go even of that understanding, that pride, that security, that sense of ground. The antidote that you're being asked to liberate is shunyata itself. Let go of even the notion of emptiness, openness, or space.

There was a crazy-wisdom teacher in India named Saraha. He said that those who believe that everything is solid and real are stupid, like cattle, but that those who believe that everything is empty are even more stupid. Everything is changing all the time, and we keep wanting to pin it down, to fix it. So whenever you come up with a solid conclusion, let the rug be pulled out. You can pull out your own rug, and you can also let life pull it out for you.

Having the rug pulled out from under you is a big opportunity to change your fundamental pattern. It's like changing the DNA. One way to pull out your own rug is by just letting go, lightening up, being more gentle, and not making such a big deal.

This approach is very different from practicing affirmations, which has been a popular thing to do in some circles. Affirmations are like screaming that you're okay in order to overcome this whisper that you're not. That's a big contrast to actually uncovering the whisper, realizing that it's passing memory, and moving closer to all those fears and all those edgy feelings that maybe you're not okay. Well, no big deal. None of us is okay and all of us are fine. It's not just one way. We are walking, talking paradoxes.

When we contemplate all dharmas as dreams and regard all our thoughts as passing memory—labeling them, "Thinking," touching them very lightly—then things will not appear to be so monolithic. We will feel a lightening of our burden. Labeling your thoughts as "thinking" will help you see the transparency of thoughts, that things are actually very light and illusory. Every time your stream of thoughts solidifies into a heavy story line that seems to be taking you elsewhere, label that "thinking." Then you will be able to see how all the passion that's connected with these thoughts, or all the aggression or all the heartbreak, is simply passing memory. If even for a second you actually had a full experience that it was all just thought, that would be a moment of full awakening.

This is how we begin to wake up our innate ability to let go, to reconnect with shunyata, or absolute bodhichitta. Also, this is how we awaken our compassion, our heart, our innate softness, relative bodhichitta. Use the labeling and use it with great gentleness as a way to touch those solid dramas and acknowledge that you just made them all up with this conversation you're having with yourself.

When we say "Self-liberate even the antidote," that's encouragement to simply touch and then let go of whatever you come up with. Whatever bright solutions or big plans you come up with, just let them go, let them go, let them go. Whether you seem to have just uncovered the root of a whole life of misery or you're thinking of a root beer float—whatever you're thinking—let it go. When something pleasant comes up, instead of rushing around the room like a windup toy, you could just pause and notice, and let go. This technique provides a gentle approach that breaks up the solidity of thoughts and memories. If the memory was a strong one, you'll probably find that something is left behind when the words go. When that happens, you're getting closer to the heart. You're getting closer to the bodhichitta.

These thoughts that come up, they're not bad. Anyway, meditation isn't about getting rid of thoughts—you'll think forever. Nevertheless, if you follow the breath and label your thoughts, you learn to let things go. Beliefs of solidity, beliefs of emptiness, let it all go. If you learn to let things go, thoughts are no problem. But at this point, for most of us, our thoughts are very tied up with our identity, with our sense of problem and our sense of how things are.

The next absolute slogan is "Rest in the nature of alaya, the essence." We can learn to let thoughts go and just rest our mind in its natural state, in alaya, which is a word that means the open primordial basis of all phenomena. We can rest in the fundamental openness and enjoy the display of whatever arises without making such a big deal.

So if you think that everything is solid, that's one trap, and if you change that for a different belief system, that's another trap. We have to pull the rug out from our belief systems altogether. We can do that by letting go of our beliefs, and also our sense of what is right and wrong, by just going back to the simplicity and the immediacy of our present experience, resting in the nature of alaya.

4

Let the World Speak for Itself

THE LAST of the absolute bodhichitta slogans is "In postmeditation, be a child of illusion." This slogan says that when you're not formally practicing meditation—which is basically the whole rest of your life—you should be a child of illusion. This is a haunting and poetic image, not all that easy to define. The way it's phrased tends to encourage you to not define it. The idea is that your experience after you finish sitting practice could be a fresh take, an ongoing opportunity to let go and lighten up.

This slogan has a lot to do with looking out and connecting with the atmosphere, with the environment that you're in, with the quality of your experience. You realize that it's not all that solid. There's always something happening that you can't pin down with words or thoughts. It's like the first day of spring. There's a special quality about that day; it is what it is, no matter what opinion you may have of it.

When we study Buddhism, we learn about the view and the meditation as supports for encouraging us to let go of ego and just be with things as they are.

These absolute bodhichitta slogans present the view. "In postmeditation, be a child of illusion" or "Regard all dharmas as dreams" for example, are pithy reminders of an underlying way of looking at the world. You don't exactly have to be able to grasp this view, but it points you in a certain direction. The suggestion that you view the world this way—as less than solid—sows seeds and wakes up certain aspects of your being.

Both the view and the meditation are great supports. They give you something to hold on to, even though all of the teachings are about not holding on to anything. We don't just talk, we actually get down to it. That's the practice, that's the meditation. You can talk about lightening up till you're purple in the face, but then you have the opportunity to practice lightening up with the outbreath, lightening up with the labeling. There is actual practice, a method that you're given, a discipline.

The view and the meditation are encouragements to relax enough so that finally the atmosphere of your experience just begins to come to you. How things really are can't be taught; no one can give you a formula: A + B + C = enlightenment.

These supports are often likened to a raft. You need the raft to cross the river, to get to the other side; when you get over there, you leave the raft behind. That's an interesting image, but in experience it's more like the raft gives out on you in the middle of the river and you never really get to solid ground. This is what is meant by becoming a child of illusion.

The "child of illusion" image seems apt because young children seem to live in a world in which things are not so solid. You see a sense of wonder in all young children, which they later lose. This slogan encourages us to be that way again.

I read a book called *The Holographic Universe*, which is about science making the same discoveries that we make sitting in meditation. The room that we sit in is solid and very vivid; it would be ridiculous to say that it wasn't there. But what science is finding out is that the material world isn't as solid as it seems; it's more like a hologram—vivid, but empty at the same time. In fact, the more you realize the lack of solidity of things, the more vivid things appear.

Trungpa Rinpoche expresses this paradox in poetic and haunting language. To paraphrase *The Sadhana of Mahamudra*: everything you see is vividly unreal in emptiness, yet there's definitely form. What you see is not here; it's not *not* here. It's both and neither. Everything you hear is the echo of emptiness, yet there's sound—it's real—the echo of emptiness. Then Trungpa Rinpoche goes on to say, "Good and bad, happy and sad, all thoughts vanish into emptiness like the imprint of a bird in the sky."

This is as close as you could come to describing what it means to be a child of illusion. That's the key point: this good and bad, happy and sad, can be allowed to dissolve into emptiness like the imprint of a bird in the sky.

The practice and the view are supports, but the real thing—the experience of sound being like an echo of emptiness or everything you see being vividly unreal—dawns on you, like waking up out of an ancient sleep. There's no way you can force it or fake it. The view and the practice are there to be experienced with a light touch, not to be taken as dogma.

We have to listen to these slogans, chew on them, and wonder about them. We have to find out for ourselves what they mean. They are like challenges rather than statements of fact. If we let them, they will lead us toward the fact that facts themselves are very dubious. We can be a child of illusion through our waking and sleeping existence; through our birth and our death, we can continually remain as a child of illusion.

Being a child of illusion also has to do with beginning to encourage yourself not to be a walking battleground. We have such strong feelings of good and evil, right and wrong. We also feel that parts of ourselves are bad or evil and parts of ourselves are good and wholesome. All these pairs of opposites—happy and sad, victory and defeat, loss and gain—are at war with each other.

The truth is that good and bad coexist; sour and sweet coexist. They aren't really opposed to each other. We could start to open our eyes and our hearts to that deep way of perceiving, like moving into a whole new dimension of experience: becoming a child of illusion.

Maybe you've heard that the Buddha is not *out there;* the Buddha is within. The Buddha within is bad and good coexisting, evil and purity coexisting; the Buddha within is not just all the nice stuff. The Buddha within is messy as well as clean. The Buddha within is really sordid as well as wholesome—yucky, smelly, repulsive as well as the opposite: they coexist.

This view is not easy to grasp, but it's helpful to hear. At the everyday kitchen-sink level, it simply means that as you see things in yourself that you think are terrible and not worthy, maybe you could reflect that that's Buddha. You're proud of yourself because you just had a good meditation or because you're having such saintly thoughts. That's Buddha too. When we get into tonglen practice, you'll see just how interesting this logic is. Tonglen as well as basic shamatha-vipashyana practice leads us toward realizing that opposites coexist. They aren't at war with each other.

In meditation practice we struggle a lot with trying to get rid of certain things, while other things come to the front. In order for the world to speak for itself, we first have to see how hard we struggle, and then we could begin to open our hearts and minds to that fact. The view and the meditation—both shamatha-vipashyana and tonglen—are meant to support a softer, more gentle approach to the whole show, the whole catastrophe. We begin to let opposites coexist, not trying to get rid of anything but just training and opening our eyes, ears, nostrils, taste buds, hearts, and minds wider and wider, nurturing the habit of opening to whatever is occurring, including our shutting down.

We generally interpret the world so heavily in terms of good and bad, happy and sad, nice and not nice that the world doesn't get a chance to speak for itself. When we say, "Be a child of illusion," we're beginning to get at this fresh way of looking when we're not caught in our hope and fear. We become mindful, awake, and gentle with our hope and fear. We see them clearly with less bias, less judgment, less sense of a heavy trip. When this happens, the world will speak for itself.

I heard a story about Trungpa Rinpoche sitting in a garden with His Holiness Dilgo Khyentse Rinpoche. People were standing around at a distance, close enough to hear but far enough away to give them privacy and space. It was a beautiful day. These two gentlemen had been sitting in the garden for a long time, just sitting there not saying anything. Time went on, and they just sat in the garden not saying anything and seeming to enjoy it very much. Then Trungpa Rinpoche broke the silence and began to laugh. He said to Dilgo Khyentse Rinpoche, pointing across the lawn, "They call that a tree." Whereupon Khyentse Rinpoche started to laugh too. Had we been there, I think we might have had a little transmission of what it means to be a child of illusion.

We can practice this way in our postmeditation now and for the rest of our lives. Whatever we're doing, whether we're having tea or working, we could do that completely. We could be wherever we are completely, 100 percent.

Take the whole teatime just to drink your tea. I started doing this in airports. Instead of reading, I sit there and look at everything, and appreciate it. Even if you don't feel appreciation, just look. Feel what you feel; take an interest and be curious. Write less; don't try to capture it all on paper. Sometimes writing, instead of being a fresh take, is like trying to catch something and nail it down. This capturing blinds us and there's no fresh outlook, no wide-open eyes, no curiosity. When we are not trying to capture anything we become like a child of illusion.

In the morning you feel one way; in the afternoon, it can seem as if years have passed. It's just astounding how it all just keeps moving on. When you write a letter, you say, "I'm feeling crummy." But by the time the person gets the letter, it's all changed. Have you ever gotten back an answer to your letter and then thought, "What are they talking about?" You don't remember this long-forgotten identity you sent out in the mail.

There was a Native American man called Ishi, which in his language meant "person" or "human being." He was a good example of what it means to be a child of illusion. Ishi lived in northern California at the beginning of the century. Everyone in his whole tribe had been methodically killed, hunted down like coyotes and wolves. Ishi was the only one left. He had lived alone for a long time. No one knew exactly why, but one day he just appeared in Oroville, California, at dawn. There stood this naked man. They quickly put some clothes on him and put him in jail, until the Bureau of Indian Affairs told them what to do with him. It was front-page news in the San Francisco newspapers, where an anthropologist named Alfred Kroeber read the story.

Here was an anthropologist's dream come true. This native person had been living in the wilds all his life and could reveal his tribe's way of life. Ishi was brought on the train down to San Francisco into a totally unknown world, where he lived—pretty happily, it appears—for the rest of his life. Ishi seemed to be fully awake. He was completely at home with himself and the world, even when it changed so dramatically almost overnight.

For instance, when they took him to San Francisco, he happily wore the suit and tie they gave him, but he carried the shoes in his hand, because he still wanted to feel the earth with his feet. He had been living as a caveman might, always having to remain hidden for fear of being killed. But very soon after he arrived in the city they took him to a formal dinner party. He sat there unperturbed by this unfamiliar ritual, just observing, and then ate the way everybody else did. He was full of wonder, completely curious about everything, and seemingly not afraid or resentful, just totally open.

When Ishi was first taken to San Francisco, he went to the Oroville train station and stood on the platform. When the train came in, without anyone really noticing, he simply walked away very quietly and stood behind a pillar. Then the others noticed and beckoned to him, and they all got on the train to San Francisco. Later, Ishi told Kroeber that for his whole life when he and the other members of his tribe had seen that train they had thought it was a demon that ate people, because of how it snaked along and bellowed smoke and fire. When Kroeber heard that, he was awestruck. He asked, "How did you have the courage to just get on the train if you thought it was a demon?" Then Ishi said, quite simply, "Well, my life has taught me to be more curious than afraid." His life had taught him what it meant to be a child of illusion.

5

Poison as Medicine

W ITH THE SLOGAN "Three objects, three poisons, and three seeds of virtue" we begin to
enter into the teachings on relative bodhichitta, the
teachings on how to awaken compassion. We have so
far been attempting to establish that the ground of all
of our experience is very spacious, not as solid as we
tend to make it. We don't have to make such a big
deal about ourselves, our enemies, our lovers, and
the whole show. This emphasis on gentleness is the
pith instruction on how to reconnect with openness
and freshness in our lives, how to liberate ourselves
from the small world of ego. We'll keep coming back
to this sense of freshness and open space and not
making such a big deal, because we are now about to
get into the really messy stuff.

In the Buddhist teachings, the messy stuff is
called *klesha,* which means poison. Boiling it all
down to the simplest possible formula, there are
three main poisons: passion, aggression, and ignorance. We could talk about these in different ways—
for example, craving, aversion, and couldn't care less.
Addictions of all kinds come under the category of
craving, which is wanting, wanting, wanting—feel-

ing that we have to have some kind of resolution. Aversion encompasses violence, rage, hatred, and negativity of all kinds, as well as garden-variety irritation. And ignorance? Nowadays, it's usually called denial.

The pith instruction of all the Buddhist teachings and most explicitly of the lojong teachings is, whatever you do, don't try to make these unwanted feelings go away. That's an unusual thought; it's not our habitual tendency to let these feelings hang around. Our habitual tendency is definitely to try to make those things go away.

People and situations in our lives are always triggering our passion, aggression, and ignorance. A good old innocent cup of coffee triggers some people's craving; they are addicted to it; it represents comfort and all the good things in life. If they can't get it, their life is a wreck. Other people have an elaborate story line about why it's bad for you, and they have aversion and a support group. Plenty of other people couldn't care less about a cup of coffee; it doesn't mean much at all to them.

And then there's good old Mortimer, that person who is sitting next to you in the meditation hall, or perhaps someone who works in your office. Some people are lusting when they see Mortimer. He looks wonderful to them. A lot of their discursive thought is taken up with what they'd like to do with Mortimer. A certain number of people hate him. They haven't even talked to him yet, but the minute they saw him, they felt loathing. Some of us haven't noticed him, and we may never notice him. In fact, a few years from now he'll tell us he was here, and we'll be surprised.

So there are three things, which in the slogan are called three objects. One object is what we find pleasant, another is what we find unpleasant, and a third is what we're neutral about. If it's pleasant, it triggers craving; if it's unpleasant, it triggers aversion; if it's neutral, it triggers ignorance. Craving, aversion, and ignorance are the three poisons.

Our experience would write the formula as "Three objects, three poisons, and lots of misery" or "Three objects, three poisons, and three seeds of confusion, bewilderment, and pain," because the more the poisons arise and the bigger they get in our life, the more they drive us crazy. They keep us from seeing the world as it is; they make us blind, deaf, and dumb. The world doesn't speak for itself because we're so caught up in our story line that instead of feeling that there's a lot of space in which we could lead our life as a child of illusion, we're robbing ourselves, robbing ourselves from letting the world speak for itself. You just keep speaking to yourself, so nothing speaks to you.

The three poisons are always trapping you in one way or another, imprisoning you and making your world really small. When you feel craving, you could be sitting on the edge of the Grand Canyon, but all you can see is this piece of chocolate cake that you're craving. With aversion, you're sitting on the edge of the Grand Canyon, and all you can hear is the angry words you said to someone ten years ago. With ignorance, you're sitting on the edge of the Grand Canyon with a paper bag over your head. Each of the three poisons has the power to capture you so completely that you don't even perceive what's in front of you.

This "Three objects, three poisons, and three seeds of virtue" is really a peculiar idea. It turns the conventional formula on its head in an unpredictable, nonhabitual way. It points to how the three poisons can be three seeds of becoming a child of illusion, how to step out of this limited world of ego fixation, how to step out of the world of tunnel vision. And the slogan is just an introduction to how this notion works. Tonglen practice will give you a very explicit method for working with this kind of lojong logic or, you could say, big-heart logic.

There's nothing really wrong with passion or aggression or ignorance, except that we take it so personally and therefore waste all that juicy stuff. The peacock eats poison and that's what makes the colors of its tail so brilliant. That's the traditional image for this practice, that the poison becomes the source of great beauty and joy; poison becomes medicine.

Whatever you do, don't try to make the poisons go away, because if you're trying to make them go away, you're losing your wealth, along with your neurosis. All this messy stuff is your richness, but saying this once is not going to convince you. If nothing else, however, it could cause you to wonder about these teachings and begin to be curious whether they could possibly be true, which might inspire you to try them for yourself.

The main point is that when Mortimer walks by and triggers your craving or your aversion or your ignorance or your jealousy or your arrogance or your feeling of worthlessness—when Mortimer walks by and a feeling arises—that could be like a little bell going off in your head or a lightbulb going on: here's an opportunity to awaken your heart. Here's an opportunity to ripen bodhichitta, to reconnect with the sense of the soft spot, because as a result of these poisons the shields usually come up. We react to the poisons by armoring our hearts.

When the poisons arise, we counter them with two main tactics. Step one: Mortimer walks by. Step two: klesha arises. (It's hard to separate the first two steps.) Step three: we either *act out* or *repress,* which is to say we either physically or mentally attack Mortimer or talk to ourself about what a jerk he is or how we're going to get even with him, or else we repress those feelings.

Acting out and repressing are the main ways that we shield our hearts, the main ways that we never really connect with our vulnerability, our compassion, our sense of the open, fresh dimension of our being. By acting out or repressing we invite suffering, bewilderment, or confusion to intensify.

Drive all blames into Mortimer. Someone once heard the slogan "Drive all blames into one" and thought it was "Drive all blames into Juan." Whether you call him or her Juan or Juanita or Mortimer, the usual tactic is either to act out or repress. If Mortimer or Juan or Juanita walks by and craving arises, you try to get together by flirting or making advances. If aversion arises, you try to get revenge. You don't stay with the raw feelings. You don't hold your seat. You take it a step further and act out.

Repressing could actually come under the category of ignorance. When you see Juan or Juanita or Mortimer, you just shut down. Maybe you don't even want to touch what they remind you of, so you just shut down. There's another common form of repression, which has to do with guilt: Juan walks by; aversion arises; you act out; and then you feel guilty about it. You think you're a bad person to be hating Juan, and so you repress it.

What we're working with in our basic shamatha-vipashyana practice—and explicitly with the tonglen practice—is the middle ground between acting out and repressing. We're discovering how to hold our seat and feel completely what's underneath all that story line of wanting, not wanting, and so forth.

In terms of "Three objects, three poisons, and three seeds of virtue," when these poisons arise, the instruction is to drop the story line, which means—instead of acting out or repressing—use the situation as an opportunity to feel your heart, to feel the wound. Use it as an opportunity to touch that soft spot. Underneath all that craving or aversion or jealousy or feeling wretched about yourself, underneath all that hopelessness and despair and depression, there's something extremely soft, which is called bodhichitta.

When these things arise, train gradually and very gently without making it into a big deal. Begin to get the hang of feeling what's underneath the story line. Feel the wounded heart that's underneath the addiction, self-loathing, or anger. If someone comes along and shoots an arrow into your heart, it's fruitless to stand there and yell at the person. It would be much better to turn your attention to the fact that there's an arrow in your heart and to relate to that wound.

When we do that, the three poisons become three seeds of how to make friends with ourselves. They give us the chance to work on patience and kindness, the chance not to give up on ourselves and not to act out or repress. They give us the chance to change our habits completely. This is what helps both ourselves and others. This is instruction on how to turn un-

wanted circumstances into the path of enlightenment. By following it, we can transform all that
messy stuff that we usually push away into the path
of awakening: reconnecting with our soft heart, our
clarity, and our ability to open further.

6

Start Where You Are

T HERE ARE TWO SLOGANS that go along with the tonglen practice: "Sending and taking should be practiced alternately. / These two should ride the breath"—which is actually a description of tonglen and how it works—and "Begin the sequence of sending and taking with yourself."

The slogan "Begin the sequence of sending and taking with yourself" is getting at the point that compassion starts with making friends with ourselves, and particularly with our poisons—the messy areas. As we practice tonglen—taking and sending—and contemplate the lojong slogans, gradually it begins to dawn on us how totally interconnected we all are. Now people know that what we do to the rivers in South America affects the whole world, and what we do to the air in Alaska affects the whole world. Everything is interrelated—including ourselves, so this is very important, this making friends with ourselves. It's the key to a more sane, compassionate planet.

What you do for yourself—any gesture of kindness, any gesture of gentleness, any gesture of honesty and clear seeing toward yourself—will affect how you experience your world. In fact, it will transform how you experience the world. What you do for yourself, you're doing for others, and what you do for others, you're doing for yourself. When you exchange yourself for others in the practice of tonglen, it becomes increasingly uncertain what is out there and what is in here.

If you have rage and righteously act it out and blame it all on others, it's really you who suffers. The other people and the environment suffer also, but you suffer more because you're being eaten up inside with rage, causing you to hate yourself more and more.

We act out because, ironically, we think it will bring us some relief. We equate it with happiness. Often there *is* some relief, for the moment. When you have an addiction and you fulfill that addiction, there is a moment in which you feel some relief. Then the nightmare gets worse. So it is with aggression. When you get to tell someone off, you might feel pretty good for a while, but somehow the sense of righteous indignation and hatred grows, and it hurts you. It's as if you pick up hot coals with your bare hands and throw them at your enemy. If the coals happen to hit him, he will be hurt. But in the meantime, you are guaranteed to be burned.

On the other hand, if we begin to surrender to ourselves—begin to drop the story line and experience what all this messy stuff behind the story line feels like—we begin to find bodhichitta, the tenderness that's under all that harshness. By being kind to ourselves, we become kind to others. By being kind to others—if it's done properly, with proper understanding—we benefit as well. So the first point is that we are completely interrelated. What you do to others, you do to yourself. What you do to yourself, you do to others.

Start where you are. This is very important. Tonglen practice (and all meditation practice) is not about later, when you get it all together and you're this person you really respect. You may be the most violent person in the world—that's a fine place to start. That's a very rich place to start—juicy, smelly. You might be the most depressed person in the world, the most addicted person in the world, the most jealous person in the world. You might think that there are no others on the planet who hate themselves as much as you do. All of that is a good place to start. Just where you are—that's the place to start.

As we begin to practice shamatha-vipashyana meditation, following our breath and labeling our thoughts, we can gradually begin to realize how profound it is just to let those thoughts go, not rejecting them, not trying to repress them, but just simply acknowledging them as violent thoughts, thoughts of hatred, thoughts of wanting, thoughts of poverty, thoughts of loathing, whatever they might be. We can see it all as thinking and can let the thoughts go

and begin to feel what's left. We can begin to feel the
energy of our heart, our body, our neck, our head, our
stomach—that basic feeling that's underneath all of
the story lines. If we can relate directly with that,
then all of the rest is our wealth. When we don't act
out and we don't repress, then our passion, our aggression, and our ignorance become our wealth. The
poison already is the medicine. You don't have to
transform anything. Simply letting go of the story
line is what it takes, which is not that easy. That light
touch of acknowledging what we're thinking and letting it go is the key to connecting with this wealth
that we have. With all the messy stuff, no matter how
messy it is, just start where you are—not tomorrow,
not later, not yesterday when you were feeling better—but now. Start now, just as you are.

Milarepa is one of the lineage holders of the Kagyü
lineage of Tibetan Buddhism. Milarepa is one of the
heroes, one of the brave ones, a very crazy, unusual
fellow. He was a loner who lived in caves by himself
and meditated wholeheartedly for years. He was
extremely stubborn and determined. If he couldn't
find anything to eat for a couple of years, he just ate
nettles and turned green, but he would never stop
practicing.

One evening Milarepa returned to his cave after
gathering firewood, only to find it filled with demons.
They were cooking his food, reading his books, sleeping in his bed. They had taken over the joint. He knew

about nonduality of self and other, but he still didn't quite know how to get these guys out of his cave. Even though he had the sense that they were just a projection of his own mind—all the unwanted parts of himself—he didn't know how to get rid of them.

So first he taught them the dharma. He sat on this seat that was higher than they were and said things to them about how we are all one. He talked about compassion and shunyata and how poison is medicine. Nothing happened. The demons were still there. Then he lost his patience and got angry and ran at them. They just laughed at him. Finally, he gave up and just sat down on the floor, saying, "I'm not going away and it looks like you're not either, so let's just live here together."

At that point, all of them left except one. Milarepa said, "Oh, this one is particularly vicious." (We all know that one. Sometimes we have lots of them like that. Sometimes we feel that's all we've got.) He didn't know what to do, so he surrendered himself even further. He walked over and put himself right into the mouth of the demon and said, "Just eat me up if you want to." Then that demon left too. The moral of the story is, when the resistance is gone, so are the demons.

That's the underlying logic of tonglen practice and also of lojong altogether. When the resistance is gone, so are the demons. It's like a koan that we can work with by learning how to be more gentle, how to relax, and how to surrender to the situations and people in our lives.

Having said all that, now I'll talk about tonglen. I've noticed that people generally eat up the teachings, but when it comes to having to do tonglen, they say, "Oh, it sounded good, but I didn't realize you actually meant it." In its essence, this practice of tonglen is, when anything is painful or undesirable, to breathe it in. That's another way of saying you don't resist it. You surrender to yourself, you acknowledge who you are, you honor yourself. As unwanted feelings and emotions arise, you actually breathe them in and connect with what all humans feel. We all know what it is to feel pain in its many guises.

This breathing in is done for yourself, in the sense that it's a personal and real experience, but simultaneously there's no doubt that you're at the same time developing your kinship with all beings. If you can know it in yourself, you can know it in everyone. If you're in a jealous rage and it occurs to you to actually breathe it in rather than blame it on someone else— if you get in touch with the arrow in your heart—it's quite accessible to you at that very moment that there are people all over the world feeling exactly what you're feeling. This practice cuts through culture, economic status, intelligence, race, religion.

People everywhere feel pain—jealousy, anger, being left out, feeling lonely. Everybody feels that exactly the way you feel it. The story lines vary, but the underlying feeling is the same for us all.

By the same token, if you feel some sense of delight—if you connect with what for you is inspiring, opening, relieving, relaxing—you breathe it out, you give it away, you send it out to everyone else. Again, it's very personal. It starts with *your* feeling of delight, *your* feeling of connecting with a bigger perspective, *your* feeling of relief or relaxation. If you're willing to drop the story line, you feel exactly what all other human beings feel. It's shared by all of us. In this way if we do the practice personally and genuinely, it awakens our sense of kinship with all beings.

The other thing that's very important is absolute bodhichitta. In order to do tonglen, we've first established the ground of absolute bodhichitta because it's important that when you breathe in and connect with the vividness and reality of pain there's also some sense of space. There's that vast, tender, empty heart of bodhichitta, your awakened heart. Right in the pain there's a lot of room, a lot of openness. You begin to touch in on that space when you relate directly to the messy stuff, because by relating directly with the messy stuff you are completely undoing the way ego holds itself together.

We shield our heart with an armor woven out of very old habits of pushing away pain and grasping at pleasure. When we begin to breathe in the pain instead of pushing it away, we begin to open our hearts to what's unwanted. When we relate directly in this way to the unwanted areas of our lives, the airless room of ego begins to be ventilated. In the same way, when we open up our clenched hearts and let the good things go—radiate them out and share them with others—that's also completely reversing the logic of ego, which is to say, reversing the logic of suffering. Lojong logic is the logic that transcends the messy and unmessy, transcends pain and pleasure. Lojong logic begins to open up the space and it begins to ventilate this whole cocoon that we find ourselves in. Whether you are breathing in or breathing out, you are opening the heart, which is awakening bodhichitta.

So now the technique. Tonglen practice has four stages. The *first stage* is flashing openness, or flashing absolute bodhichitta. The slogan "Rest in the nature of alaya, the essence" goes along with this flash of openness, which is done very quickly. There is some sort of natural flash of silence and space. It's a very simple thing.

The *second stage* is working with the texture. You visualize breathing in dark, heavy, and hot and breathing out white, light, and cool. The idea is that you are always breathing in the same thing: you are essentially breathing in the cause of suffering, the origin of suffering, which is fixation, the tendency to hold on to ego with a vengeance.

You may have noticed, when you become angry or poverty-stricken or jealous, that you experience that fixation as black, hot, solid, and heavy. That is actually the texture of poison, the texture of neurosis and fixation. You may have also noticed times when you are all caught up in yourself, and *then* some sort of contrast or gap occurs. It's very spacious. That's the experience of mind that is not fixated on phenomena; it's the experience of openness. The texture of that openness is generally experienced as light, white, fresh, clear, and cool.

So in the second stage of tonglen you work with those textures. You breathe in black, heavy, and hot through all the pores of your body, and you radiate out white, light, and cool, also through all the pores of your body, 360 degrees. You work with the texture until you feel that it's synchronized: black is coming in and white is going out on the medium of the breath—in and out, in and out.

The *third stage* is working with a specific heartfelt object of suffering. You breathe in the pain of a specific person or animal that you wish to help. You breathe out to that person spaciousness or kindness or a good meal or a cup of coffee—whatever you feel would lighten their load. You can do this for anyone: the homeless mother that you pass on the street, your suicidal uncle, or yourself and the pain you are feeling at that very moment. The main point is that the suffering is real, totally untheoretical. It should be heartfelt, tangible, honest, and vivid.

The *fourth stage* extends this wish to relieve suffering much further. You start with the homeless person and then extend out to all those who are suffering just as she is, or to all those who are suicidal like your uncle or to all those who are feeling the jealousy or addiction or contempt that you are feeling. You use specific instances of misery and pain as a stepping stone for understanding the universal suffering of people and animals everywhere. Simultaneously, you breathe in the pain of your uncle and of all the zillions of other desperate, lonely people like him. Simultaneously, you send out spaciousness or cheerfulness or a bunch of flowers, whatever would be healing, to your uncle and all the others. What you feel for one person, you can extend to all people.

You need to work with both the third and fourth stages—with both the immediate suffering of one person and the universal suffering of all. If you were only to extend out to all sentient beings, the practice would be very theoretical. It would never actually touch your heart. On the other hand, if you were to work only with your own or someone else's fixation, it would lack vision. It would be too narrow. Working with both situations together makes the practice real and heartfelt; at the same time, it provides vision and a way for you to work with everyone else in the world.

You can bring all of your unfinished karmic business right into the practice. In fact, you should invite it in. Suppose that you are involved in a horrific relationship: every time you think of a particular person you get *furious*. That is very useful for tonglen! Or perhaps you feel depressed. It was all you could do to get out of bed today. You're so depressed that you want to stay in bed for the rest of your life; you have considered hiding *under* your bed. That is very useful for tonglen practice. The specific fixation should be *real*, just like that.

Let's use another example. You may be formally doing tonglen or just sitting having your coffee, and here comes Mortimer, the object of your passion, aggression, or ignorance. You want to hit him or hug him, or maybe you wish that he weren't there at all.

But let's say you're angry. The object is Mortimer and here comes the poison: *fury*. You breathe that in. The idea is to develop sympathy for your own confusion. The technique is that you do not blame Mortimer; you also do not blame yourself. Instead, there is just liberated fury—hot, black, and heavy. Experience it as fully as you can.

You breathe the anger in; you remove the object; you stop thinking about him. In fact, he was just a useful catalyst. Now you own the anger completely. You drive all blames into yourself. It takes a lot of bravery, and it's extremely insulting to ego. In fact, it destroys the whole mechanism of ego. So you breathe in.

Then, you breathe out sympathy, relaxation, and spaciousness. Instead of just a small, dark situation, you allow a lot of space for these feelings. Breathing out is like ventilating the whole thing, airing it out. Breathing out is like opening up your arms and just letting go. It's fresh air. Then you breathe the rage in again—the black, heavy hotness of it. Then you breathe out, ventilating the whole thing, allowing a lot of space.

What you are actually doing is cultivating kindness toward yourself. It is very simple in that way. You don't think about it; you don't philosophize; you simply breathe in a very real klesha. You own it completely and then aerate it, allowing a lot of space when you breathe out. This, in itself, is an amazing practice—even if it didn't go any further—because at this level you are still working on yourself. But the real beauty of the practice is that you then extend that out.

Without pretending, you can acknowledge that about two billion other sentient beings are feeling the exact same rage that you are at that moment. They are experiencing it exactly the way you are experiencing it. They may have a different object, but the object isn't the point. The point is the rage itself. You breathe it in from all of them, so they no longer have to have it. It doesn't make your own rage any greater; it is just rage, just fixation on rage, which causes so much suffering.

Sometimes, at that moment, you get a glimpse of why there is murder and rape, why there is war, why people burn down buildings, why there is so much misery in the world. It all comes from feeling that rage and acting it out instead of taking it in and airing it. It all turns into hatred and misery, which pollutes the world and obviously perpetuates the vicious cycle of suffering and frustration. Because *you* feel rage, therefore you have the kindling, the connection, for understanding the rage of all sentient beings. First you work with your own klesha; then you quickly extend that and breathe it all in.

At that point, simultaneously, it is no longer *your* own particular burden; it is just the rage of sentient beings, which includes you. You breathe that in, and you breathe out a sense of ventilation, so that all sentient beings could experience that. This goes for anything that bothers you. The more it bothers you, the more awake you're going to be when you do tonglen.

The things that really drive us nuts have enormous energy in them. That is why we fear them. It could even be your own timidity: you are so timid that you are afraid to walk up and say hello to someone, afraid to look someone in the eye. It takes a lot of energy to maintain that. It's the way you keep yourself together.

In tonglen practice, you have the chance to own that completely, not blaming anybody, and to ventilate it with the outbreath. Then you might better understand why some other people in the room look so grim: it isn't because they hate you but because they feel the same kind of timidity and don't want to look anyone in the face. In this way, the tonglen practice is both a practice of making friends with yourself and a practice of compassion.

By practicing in this way, you definitely develop your sympathy for others, and you begin to understand them a lot better. In that way your own pain is like a stepping stone. Your heart develops more and more, and even if someone comes up and insults you, you could genuinely understand the whole situation because you understand so well where everybody's coming from. You also realize that you can help by simply breathing *in* the pain of others and breathing *out* that ventilation. So tonglen starts with relating directly to specific suffering—yours or someone else's—which you then use to understand that this suffering is universal, shared by us all.

Almost everybody can begin to do tonglen by thinking of someone he or she loves very dearly. It's sometimes easier to think of your children than your husband or wife or mother or father, because those relationships may be more complicated. There are some people in your life whom you love very straightforwardly without complication: old people or people who are ill or little children, or people who have been kind to you.

When he was eight years old, Trungpa Rinpoche saw a whimpering puppy being stoned to death by a laughing, jeering crowd. He said that after that, doing tonglen practice was straightforward for him: all he had to do was think of that dog and his heart would start to open instantly. There was nothing complicated about it. He would have done anything to breathe in the suffering of that animal and to breathe out relief. So the idea is to start with something like that, something that activates your heart.

So you think of a puppy being stoned and dying in pain, and you breathe that in. Then, it is no longer just a puppy. It is your connection with the realization that there are puppies and people suffering unjustly like that all over the world. You immediately extend the practice and breathe in the suffering of all the people who are suffering like that animal.

It is also possible to start with the puppy or your uncle or yourself and then gradually extend out further and further. Having started with the wish to relieve your sister's depression, you could extend further and breathe in the depression of people who are somewhat "neutral"—the ones to whom you are not that close but who also don't cause you fear or anger. You breathe in the depression and send out relief to all those "neutral" people. Then, gradually, the practice moves to people you actually *hate,* people you consider to be your enemies or to have actually harmed you. This expansion evolves by doing the practice. You cannot fake these things; therefore you start with the things that are close to your heart.

It's useful to think of tonglen practice in four stages:

1. Flashing openness
2. Working with the texture, breathing in dark, heavy, and hot and breathing out white, light, and cool
3. Working with relieving a specific, heartfelt instance of suffering
4. Extending that wish to help everyone

The main thing is to really get in touch with fixation and the power of klesha activity in yourself. This makes other people's situations completely accessible and real to you. Then, when it becomes real and vivid, always remember to extend it out. Let your own experience be a stepping stone for working with the world.

7

Bringing All That We Meet to the Path

Today's slogan is "When the world is filled with evil, / Transform all mishaps into the path of bodhi." The word *bodhi* means "enlightenment." This is the basic statement of lojong altogether: how to use the unwanted, unfavorable circumstances of your life as the actual material of awakening. This is the precious gift of the lojong teachings, that whatever occurs isn't considered an interruption or an obstacle but a way to wake up. This slogan is very well suited to our busy lives and difficult times. In fact, it's designed for that: if there were no difficulties, there would be no need for lojong or tonglen.

Bodhisattva is another word for the awakening warrior, the one who cultivates bravery and compassion. One point this slogan is making is that on the path of the warrior, or bodhisattva, there is no interruption. The path includes all experience, both serene and chaotic. When things are going well, we feel good. We delight in the beauty of the snow falling outside the windows or the light reflecting off the floor. There's some sense of appreciation. But when the fire alarm rings and confusion erupts, we feel irritated and upset.

It's all opportunity for practice. There is no interruption. We would like to believe that when things are still and calm, that's the real stuff, and when things are messy, confused, and chaotic, we've done something wrong, or more usually someone *else* has done something to ruin our beautiful meditation. As someone once said about a loud, bossy woman, "What is that woman doing in my sacred world?"

Another point about this slogan is that part of awakening is to cultivate honesty and clear seeing. Sometimes people take the lojong teachings to mean that if you're not to blame others but instead to connect with the feelings beneath your own story line, it would be wrong to say that someone has harmed you. However, part of honesty, clear seeing, and straightforwardness is being able to acknowledge that harm has been done. The first noble truth—the very first teaching of the Buddha—is that there is suffering. Suffering does exist as part of the human experience. People harm each other—we harm others and others harm us. To know that is clear seeing.

This is tricky business. What's the difference between seeing that harm has been done and blaming? Perhaps it is that rather than point the finger of blame, we raise questions: "How can I communicate? How can I help the harm that has been done unravel itself? How can I help others find their own wisdom, kindness, and sense of humor?" That's a much greater challenge than blaming and hating and acting out.

How can we help? The way that we can help is by making friends with our own feelings of hatred, bewilderment, and so forth. Then we can accept them in others. With this practice you begin to realize that you're capable of playing all the parts. It's not just "them"; it's "us" *and* "them."

I used to feel outrage when I read about parents abusing their children, particularly physically. I used to get righteously indignant—until I became a mother. I remember very clearly one day, when my six-month-old son was screaming and crying and covered in oatmeal and my two-and-a-half-year-old daughter was pulling on me and knocking things off the table, thinking, "I understand why all those mothers hurt their children. I understand perfectly. It's only that I've been brought up in a culture that doesn't encourage me that way, so I'm not going to do it. But at this moment, everything in me wants to eradicate completely these two sweet little children."

So lest you find yourself condescendingly doing tonglen for the other one who's *so* confused, you could remember that this is a practice where compassion begins to arise in you because you yourself have been there. You've been angry, jealous, and lonely. You know what it's like and you know how sometimes you do strange things. Because you're lonely, you say cruel words; because you want someone to love you, you insult them. Exchanging yourself for others begins to occur when you can see where someone is because you've been there. It doesn't happen because you're better than they are but because human beings share the same stuff. The more you know your own, the more you're going to understand others.

When the world is filled with evil, how do we transform unwanted situations into the path of awakening? One way is to flash absolute bodhichitta. But most of the techniques have to do with relative bodhichitta, which is to say, awakening our connection with the soft spot, reconnecting with the soft spot, not only through the stuff we like but also through the messy stuff.

People have plenty of reasons to be angry. We have to acknowledge this. We are angry. But blaming the other doesn't solve anything.

Ishi had plenty of reasons to be angry. His whole tribe had been killed, methodically, one by one. There was no one left but him. But he wasn't angry. We could learn a lesson from him. No matter what's happening, if we can relate to the soft spot that's underneath our rage and can connect with what's there, then we can relate to the enemy in a way in which we can start to be able to exchange ourself for other. Some sense of being able to communicate with the enemy—heart to heart—is the only way that things can change. As long as we hate the enemy, then we suffer and the enemy suffers and the world suffers.

The only way to effect real reform is without hatred. This is the message of Martin Luther King, of Cesar Chavez, of Mother Teresa. Gerald Red Elk—a close friend and teacher who was a Sioux elder—told me that as a young man he had been filled with hatred for how his people had been, and continue to be, treated. Because of his hatred, he was alcoholic and miserable. But during the Second World War, when he was in Europe, something in him shifted; he saw that he was being poisoned by his hatred. He came back from the war, and for the rest of his life he tried to bring back the sense of spirit and confidence and dignity of the young people in his tribe. His main message was not to hate but to learn to communicate with all beings. He had a very big mind.

Another slogan says, "All dharma agrees at one point." No matter what the teachings are—shamatha-vipashyana instruction, lojong instruction, any instruction of sanity and health from any tradition of wisdom—the point at which they all agree is to let go of holding on to yourself. That's the way of becoming at home in your world. This is not to say that ego is sin. Ego is not sin. Ego is not something that you get rid of. Ego is something that you come to know—something that you befriend by not acting out or repressing all the feelings that you feel.

Whether we're talking about the painful international situation or our painful domestic situation, the pain is a result of what's called ego clinging, of wanting things to work out on our own terms, of wanting "me-victorious."

Ego is like a room of your own, a room with a view, with the temperature and the smells and the music that you like. You want it your own way. You'd just like to have a little peace; you'd like to have a little happiness, you know, just "gimme a break!"

But the more you think that way, the more you try to get life to come out so that it will always suit you, the more your fear of other people and what's outside your room grows. Rather than becoming more relaxed, you start pulling down the shades and locking the door. When you do go out, you find the experience more and more unsettling and disagreeable. You become touchier, more fearful, more irritable than ever. The more you just try to get it your way, the less you feel at home.

To begin to develop compassion for yourself and others, you have to unlock the door. You don't open it yet, because you have to work with your fear that somebody you don't like might come in. Then as you begin to relax and befriend those feelings, you begin to open it. Sure enough, in come the music and the smells that you don't like. Sure enough, someone puts a foot in and tells you you should be a different religion or vote for someone you don't like or give money that you don't want to give.

Now you begin to relate with those feelings. You develop some compassion, connecting with the soft spot. You relate with what begins to happen when you're not protecting yourself so much. Then gradually, like Ishi, you become more curious than afraid. To be fearless isn't really to overcome fear, it's to come to know its nature. Just open the door more and more and at some point you'll feel capable of inviting all sentient beings as your guests.

It helps to realize that the Nelson Mandelas and Mother Teresas of the world also know how it feels to be in a small room with the windows and doors closed. They also know anger and jealousy and loneliness. They're people who made friends with themselves and therefore made friends with the world. They're people who developed the bravery to be able to relate to the shaky, tender, fearful feelings in their own hearts and therefore are no longer afraid of those feelings when they are triggered by the outside world.

When you begin to practice this way, you're so honest about what you're feeling that it begins to create a sense of understanding other people as well. A young man told this story in a discussion group during a lojong training weekend. He had gone into a bar in Los Angeles to play pool. Before starting to play, he put his brand-new leather jacket down on a chair.

When he finished playing, it wasn't there. The four other people in the bar were just sitting there looking at him with big smug smiles on their faces. They were really big guys. He felt extremely small and powerless. He knew that they had taken his jacket and that it wouldn't be wise to confront them because he was small and outnumbered. He felt humiliated and helpless.

Then, as a result of having worked with this practice, it occurred to him that he could feel empathy for people in the world who had been laughed at, scorned, and spat upon because of their religion or the color of their skin or their gender or their sexual orientation or their nationality, or for whatever reason. He found himself empathizing with all the people throughout time who had found themselves in humiliating situations. It was a profound experience for him. It didn't get him his jacket back; it didn't solve anything. But it opened his heart to a lot of people with whom he had not before had any sense of shared experience.

This is where the heart comes from in this practice, where the sense of gratitude and appreciation for our life comes from. We become part of a lineage of people who have cultivated their bravery throughout history, people who, against enormous odds, have stayed open to great difficulties and painful situations and transformed them into the path of awakening. We *will* fall flat on our faces again and again, we *will* continue to feel inadequate, and we can use these experiences to wake up, just as they did. The lojong teachings give us the means to connect with the power of our lineage, the lineage of gentle warriorship.

8

Drive All Blames into One

I'D LIKE TO TALK A BIT about another slogan, "Drive all blames into one." When we say, as in a previous slogan, "When the world is filled with evil," we mean, "When the world is filled with the results of ego clinging." When the world is filled with ego clinging or with attachment to a particular outcome, there is a lot of pain. But these painful situations can be transformed into the path of bodhi. One of the ways to do that is to drive all blames into one. To see how this works, let's look at the result of blaming others.

I had someone buy me the *New York Times* on Sunday so I could look at the result of people blaming others. In Yugoslavia, there's a very painful situation. The Croats and the Serbs are murdering each other, raping each other, killing children and old people. If you asked someone on either side what they wanted, they would say they just want to be happy. The Serbs just want to be happy. They see the others as enemies and they think the only way to be happy is to eradicate the source of their misery. We all think this way. And then if you talked to the other side, they would say that they want the same thing.

This is true in Israel with the Arabs and the Jews. This is true in Northern Ireland with the Protestants and the Catholics. The same is true everywhere, and it's getting worse. In every corner of the world, the same is true.

When we look at the world in this way we see that it all comes down to the fact that no one is ever encouraged to feel the underlying anxiety, the underlying edginess, the underlying soft spot, and therefore we think that blaming others is the only way. Reading just one newspaper, we can see that blaming others doesn't work.

We have to look at our own lives as well: How are we doing with our Juans and Juanitas? Often they're the people with whom we have the most intimate relationships. They really get to us because we can't just shake them off by moving across town or changing seats on the bus, or whatever we have the luxury of doing with mere acquaintances, whom we also loathe.

The point is that if we think there is any difference between how we relate with the people who irritate us and the situation in Northern Ireland, Yugoslavia, the Middle East, or Somalia, we're wrong. If we think there is any difference between that and the way that native people feel about white people or white people feel about black people or any of these situations on earth, we're wrong. We have to start with ourselves. If all people on the planet would start with themselves, we might see quite a shift in the aggressive energy that's causing such a widespread holocaust.

"Drive all blames into one"—or "Take the blame yourself," if you prefer—sounds like a masochistic slogan. It sounds like, "Just beat me up, just bury me under piles of manure, just let me have it and kick me in the teeth." However, that isn't what it really means, you'll be happy to know.

One way of beginning to practice "Drive all blames into one" is to begin to notice what it feels like when you blame someone else. What's actually under all that talking and conversation about how wrong somebody or something is? What does blame feel like in your stomach? When we do this noticing we see that we are somehow beginning to cultivate bravery as well as compassion and honesty. When these really unresolved issues of our lives come up, we are no longer trying to escape but are beginning to be curious and open toward these parts of ourselves.

"Drive all blames into one" is a healthy and compassionate instruction that short-circuits the overwhelming tendency we have to blame everybody else; it doesn't mean, instead of blaming the other people, blame yourself. It means to touch in with what blame feels like altogether. Instead of guarding yourself, instead of pushing things away, begin to get in touch with the fact that there's a very soft spot under all that armor, and blame is probably one of the most well-perfected armors that we have.

You can take this slogan beyond what we think of as "blame" and practice applying it simply to the general sense that something is wrong. When you feel that something is wrong, let the story line go and touch in on what's underneath. You may notice that when you let the words go, when you stop talking to yourself, there's something left, and that something tends to be very soft. At first it may seem intense and vivid, but if you don't recoil from that and you keep opening your heart, you find that underneath all of the fear is what has been called shaky tenderness.

The truth of the matter is that even though there are teachings and practice techniques, still we each have to find our own way. What does it really mean to open? What does it mean not to resist? What does it mean? It's a lifetime journey to find the answers to these questions for yourself. But there's a lot of support in these teachings and this practice.

Try dropping the object of the blame or the object of what you think is wrong. Instead of throwing the snowballs out there, just put the snowball down and relate in a nonconceptual way to your anger, relate to your righteous indignation, relate to your sense of being fed up or pissed off or whatever it is. If Mortimer or Juan or Juanita walks by, instead of talking to yourself for the next four days about them, you would stop talking to yourself. Simply follow the instruction that you're given, notice that you are talking to yourself, and let it go. This is basic shamatha-vipashyana instruction—that's what it means by dropping the object. Then you can do tonglen.

If you aren't feeding the fire of anger or the fire of craving by talking to yourself, then the fire doesn't have anything to feed on. It peaks and passes on. It's said that everything has a beginning, middle, and end, but when we start blaming and talking to ourselves, things seem to have a beginning, a middle, and no end.

Strangely enough, we blame others and put so much energy into the object of anger or whatever it is because we're afraid that this anger or sorrow or loneliness is going to last forever. Therefore, instead of relating directly with the sorrow or the loneliness or the anger, we think that the way to end it is to blame it on somebody else. We might just talk to ourselves about them, or we might actually hit them or fire them or yell. Whether we're using our body, speech, mind—or all three—whatever we might do, we think, curiously enough, that this will make the pain go away. Instead, acting it out is what makes it last.

"Drive all blames into one" is saying, instead of always blaming the other, *own* the feeling of blame, *own* the anger, *own* the loneliness, and make friends with it. Use the tonglen practice to see how you can place the anger or the fear or the loneliness in a cradle of loving-kindness; use tonglen to learn how to be gentle to all that stuff. In order to be gentle and create an atmosphere of compassion for yourself, it's necessary to stop talking to yourself about how wrong everything is—or how right everything is, for that matter.

I challenge you to experiment with dropping the object of your emotion, doing tonglen, and seeing if in fact the intensity of the so-called poison lessens. I have experimented with this, because I didn't believe that it would work. I thought it couldn't possibly be true, and because my doubt was so strong, for a while it seemed to me that it didn't work. But as my trust grew, I found that that's what happens—the intensity of the klesha lessens, and so does the duration. This happens because the ego begins to be ventilated. This big solid me—"*I* have a problem. *I* am lonely. *I* am angry. *I* am addicted"—begins somehow to be aerated when you just go against the grain and own the feelings yourself instead of blaming the other.

The "one" in "Drive all blames into one" is the tendency we have to want to protect ourselves: ego clinging. When we drive all blames into this tendency by owning our feelings and feeling fully, the ongoing monolithic ME begins to lighten up, because it is fabricated with our opinions, our moods, and a lot of ephemeral, but at the same time vivid and convincing, stuff.

I know a fifteen-year-old Hispanic guy from Los Angeles. He grew up in a violent neighborhood and was in gangs from the age of thirteen. He was really smart, and curiously enough, his name was Juan. He came on really mean. He was tough and he snarled and he walked around with a big chip on his shoulder. You had the feeling that that was all he had going for him: his world was so rough that acting like the baddest and the meanest was the only way he saw to survive in it.

He was one of those people who definitely drive all blames into others. If you asked him a simple question, he would tell you to fuck off. If he could get anybody in trouble, he definitely would do so. From one point of view, he was a total pain in the neck, but on the other hand, he had a flair and brilliance about him. It was always mixed; you hated him and you loved him. He was outrageous and also sparky and funny, but he was mean—he would slap people and push them around. You knew that that was pretty lightweight compared with what he was used to doing at home, where they killed each other on a regular basis.

He was sent to Boulder, Colorado, for the summer to give him a break, to give him a nice summer in the Rocky Mountains. His mother and others were trying to help him get a good education and somehow step out of the nightmare world into which he had been born. The people he was staying with were loosely affiliated with the Buddhist community, and that's how I came to know him. One day he came to an event where Trungpa Rinpoche was, and at the end of this event, Trungpa Rinpoche sang the Shambhala anthem. This was an awful experience for the rest of us because for some reason he loved to sing the Shambhala anthem in a high-pitched, squeaky, and cracked voice.

This particular event was outside. As Rinpoche sang into a microphone and the sound traveled for miles across the plains, Juan broke down and started to cry. Everyone else was feeling awkward or embarrassed, but Juan just started to cry. Later he said he cried because he had never seen anyone that brave. He said, "That guy, he's not afraid to be a fool." That turned out to be a major turning point in his life because he realized that he didn't have to be afraid to be a fool either. All that persona and chip on the shoulder were guarding his soft spot, and he could let them go. Because he was so sharp and bright, he got the message. His life turned around. Now he's got his education and he's back in L.A. helping kids.

So that's the point, that we tend to drive all blames into Juan because Juan is so obnoxious. We aren't encouraged to get in touch with what's underneath all our words of hatred, craving, and jealousy. We just act them out again and again. But if we practice this slogan and drive all blames into *one,* the armor of our ego clinging will weaken and the soft spot in our hearts will appear. We may feel foolish, but we don't have to be afraid of that. We can make friends with ourselves.

9

Be Grateful to Everyone

T HE SLOGAN "Be grateful to everyone" is about making peace with the aspects of ourselves that we have rejected. Through doing that, we also make peace with the people we dislike. More to the point, being around people we dislike is often a catalyst for making friends with ourselves. Thus, "Be grateful to everyone."

If we were to make a list of people we don't like— people we find obnoxious, threatening, or worthy of contempt—we would find out a lot about those aspects of ourselves that we can't face. If we were to come up with one word about each of the trouble- makers in our lives, we would find ourselves with a list of descriptions of our own rejected qualities, which we project onto the outside world. The people who repel us unwittingly show us the aspects of our- selves that we find unacceptable, which otherwise we can't see. In traditional teachings on lojong it is put another way: other people trigger the karma that we haven't worked out. They mirror us and give us the chance to befriend all of that ancient stuff that we carry around like a backpack full of granite boulders.

"Be grateful to everyone" is a way of saying that we

can learn from any situation, especially if we practice this slogan with awareness. The people and situations in our lives can remind us to catch neurosis as neurosis, to see when we're in our room under the covers, to see when we've pulled the shades, locked the door, and are determined to stay there.

There's a reason that you can learn from everything: you have basic wisdom, basic intelligence, and basic goodness. Therefore, if the environment is supportive and encourages you to be brave and to open your heart and mind, you'll find yourself opening to the wisdom and compassion that's inherently there. It's like tapping into your source, tapping into what you already have. It's the willingness to open your eyes, your heart, and your mind, to allow situations in your life to become your teacher. With awareness, you are able to find out for yourself what causes misery and what causes happiness.

"Be grateful to everyone" is getting at a complete change of attitude. This slogan is not wishy-washy and naive. It does not mean that if you're mugged on the street you should smile knowingly and say, "Oh, I should be grateful for this," before losing consciousness. This slogan actually gets at the guts of how we perfect ignorance through avoidance, not knowing that we're eating poison, not knowing that we're putting another layer of protection over our heart, not seeing through the whole thing.

"Be grateful to everyone" means that all situations

teach you, and often it's the tough ones that teach you best. There may be a Juan or Juanita in your life, and Juan or Juanita is the one who gets you going. They're the ones who don't go away: your mother, your husband, your wife, your lover, your child, the person that you have to work with every single day, part of the situation you can't escape.

These situations really teach you because there's no pat solution to the problem. You're continually meeting your match. You're always coming into a challenge, coming up against your edge. There's no way that someone else can tell you exactly what to do, because you're the only one who knows where it's torturing you, where your relationship with Juan or Juanita is getting into your guts. Others don't know. They don't know when you need to be more gentle, when you need to be more clear, when you need to be quiet, and when you need to speak.

No one else knows what it takes for another person to open the door. For some people, speaking out is opening the door a little wider; for other people, being still is opening the door a little wider. It all has to do with what your ancient habitual reaction is to being in a tight spot and what is going to soften the whole thing and cause you to have a change of attitude. It's the Juans and Juanitas who present us with these dilemmas, these challenges.

Basically the only way you can communicate with the Juans and Juanitas in your life is by taking the

teachings and the practice very personally, not trusting anybody else's interpretations, because you yourself have the wisdom within, and you yourself will
find out how to open that door. As much as we would
like Juan or Juanita to get out of our life and give us a
break, somehow they stick around, and even if we do
manage to get rid of them, they seem to reappear
with another name and another face very soon. They
are addressing the point at which we are most stuck.

It's important, in terms of being grateful to everyone, to realize that no slogan, no meditation practice,
nothing that you can hear in the teachings is a solution. We're evolving. We will always be learning more
and more, continually opening further and further.

It is good to open your mind so that each situation
is completely fresh. It's as if you've never been there
before, a completely new take. But even with this approach, you can get trapped. Let's say you're a meditation instructor. Your student arrives for a meeting,
and because you're very open and in tune, something
magical happens. There's some real communication
between the two of you, and you can see that something has helped, something has gotten through and
connected with her own heart. She leaves and you
feel great—"Wow! I did that wonderful thing. I could
feel it." The next person comes in and you forget
about the freshness because you're feeling so good
about what you just did. He sits down and talks to
you and you come out with the same answers that

you just gave the last person. But that just leaves this new person cold; he couldn't care less. You have the humbling experience of realizing that there's never just one solution to a problem. Helping yourself or someone else has to do with opening and just being there; that's how something happens between people. But it's a continuous process. That's how you learn. You can't open just once.

What you learn from the Juans and Juanitas in your life is not something that you can get a patent on and then sell as a sure thing that will always work. It isn't like that. This kind of learning is a continual journey of wakefulness.

A meditation student I was working with whom I'll call Dan had a serious alcohol and drug problem. He was really making great strides, and then he went on a binge. On the day I found out about it I happened to have an opportunity to see Trungpa Rinpoche. I blurted out to him how upset I was that Dan had gone on a binge. I was so disappointed. Well, Rinpoche got really angry; it completely stopped my heart and mind. He said that being upset about Dan's binge was my problem. "You should never have expectations for other people. Just be kind to them," he told me. In terms of Dan, I should just help him keep walking forward inch by inch and be kind to him— invite him for dinner, give him little gifts, and do anything to bring some happiness to his life—instead of having these big goals for him. He said that setting goals for others can be aggressive—really wanting a success story for ourselves. When we do this to others, we are asking them to live up to our ideals. Instead, we should just be kind.

The main point of "Be grateful to everyone"—the "dig"—is that you want to get rid of the situations that drive you most crazy, the Juans and Juanitas. You don't want to be grateful to them. You want to solve the problem and not hurt anymore. Juan is making you feel embarrassed, or degraded, or abused; there's something about the way he treats you that makes you feel so bad that you just want *out*.

This slogan encourages you to realize that when you've met your match you've found a teacher. That doesn't necessarily mean that you shut up and don't say anything and just stand there breathing in and out, although that might be exactly what you do. But tonglen is much more profound than that. It has to do with how you open in this situation so that the basic goodness of Juan or Juanita and your own basic goodness begin to communicate.

Something between repressing and acting out is what's called for, but it is unique and different each time. People have the wisdom to find it. Juan and Juanita have the wisdom, you have the wisdom, everyone has the wisdom to know how to open. It's inherent in all of us. The path of not being caught in ego is a process of surrendering to situations in order to communicate rather than win.

Compassionate action, compassionate speech, is not a one-shot deal; it's a lifetime journey. But it seems to begin with realizing that when Juan or Juanita is getting to you, pushing every button, it's not as simplistic as just eating it, just becoming a worm, "Okay, let them attack me." On the other hand, it's not as easy as just saying, "I'll get *him*." It's a challenge. This is how the koan appears in everyday life: the unanswerable questions of our lives are the greatest teachers.

When the great Indian Buddhist teacher Atisha went to Tibet, he had been practicing the lojong teachings for some time. Like most practitioners, he had the feeling of being haunted by the fact that there are blind places that you don't know about. You don't know that you're stuck in certain places. So he valued the Juans and Juanitas in his life tremendously because he felt they were the only ones who got through to him enough to show him where his blind spots were. Through them his ego got smaller. Through them his compassion increased.

The story goes that Atisha was told that the people of Tibet were very good-natured, earthy, flexible, and open; he decided they wouldn't be irritating enough to push his buttons. So he brought along with him a mean-tempered, ornery Bengali tea boy. He felt that was the only way he could stay awake. The Tibetans like to tell the story that, when he got to Tibet, he realized he need not have brought his tea boy: the people there were not as pleasant as he had been told.

In our own lives, the Bengali tea boys are the people who, when you let them through the front door of your house, go right down to the basement where you store lots of things you'd rather not deal with, pick out one of them, bring it up to you, and say, "Is this yours?"

These are the people who, when your habitual style is working just fine and everyone's agreeing with you, say, "No way am I going to go along with what you just asked me to do. I think it's stupid." You think, "What do I do now?" And usually what you do is to get everybody else on your team. You sit around and talk about what a creep this person is who confronted you. If the disagreement happens to be in the realm of politics or "isms" of any kind, you get a banner on which you write how right you are and how wrong this other person is. By this time the other person has got a team, too, and then you have race riots and World War III. Righteous indignation becomes a creed for you and your whole gang. And it all started because somebody blew your trip. It all turns into a crusade of who's right and who's wrong. Wars come from that. Nobody ever encourages you to allow yourself to feel wounded first and then try to figure out what is the right speech and right action that might follow.

Gurdjieff—a teacher in the early part of the twen-

tieth century, kind of a crazy-wisdom character—
knew the meaning of this slogan. He was living not
too far from Paris in a big manor house with huge
lawns. All of his students came there to study with
him. One of his main teachings was to be awake to
whatever process you're going through. He liked to
tighten the screws on his students. In fact, it's said
that he would make you take the job that you most
didn't want to take; if you thought you should be a
college professor, he would make you become a used
car salesman.

There was a man in the community who was really
bad tempered. He was everybody's Juan; nobody
could stand this guy because he was so prickly. Every
little thing caused him to spin off into a tantrum.
Everything irritated him. He complained constantly,
so everyone felt the need to tiptoe around him because anything that might be said could cause him to
explode. People just wished that he would go away.

Gurdjieff liked to make his students do things that
were completely meaningless. One day there were
about forty people out cutting up a lawn into little
pieces and moving it to another place on the grounds.
This was too much for this fellow; it was the last
straw. He blew up, stormed out, got in his car, and
drove off, whereupon there was a spontaneous cele-
bration. People were thrilled, so happy he had gone.
But when they told Gurdjieff what had happened, he
said, "Oh no!" and went after him in his car.

Three days later they both came back. That night when Gurdjieff's attendant was serving him his supper, he asked, "Sir, why did you bring him back?" Gurdjieff answered in a very low voice, "You're not going to believe this, and this is just between you and me; you must tell no one. I pay him to stay here."

I told that story at a meditation center, and later they wrote me a letter saying, "We used to have two people here helping and there was a lot of harmony. Now we have four and the trouble is beginning. So every day we ask each other, 'Is somebody paying you to be here?'"

1 0

Cutting the Solidity
of Thoughts

I ONCE HAD AN INTERVIEW with a student who began by saying, "This is all pretty depressing, isn't it? There's something sort of grim and discouraging about what we're doing here. Where's the joy? Where's the cheerfulness in all of this?" We talked for a while. Then at the end of the interview, she had her own insight, "I guess the joy comes from getting real."

That really struck me. Whether it's connecting with the genuine heart of sadness and the messy areas of our lives, or connecting with vision and expansion and openness, what's real is all included in well-being; it's all included in joy. Joy is not about pleasure as opposed to pain or cheerfulness as opposed to sadness. Joy includes everything.

There's a slogan that says, "Don't wallow in self-pity." That's a good one to remember if you find that tonglen practice has you crying a lot. This whole approach could evolve into self-pity easily, and self-pity takes a lot of maintenance. You have to talk to yourself quite a bit to keep it up. The slogan is saying to get to know what self-pity feels like underneath the story line. That's how the training develops a genuine, openhearted, intelligent relationship with the whole variety of human experience.

We're so funny: the people who are crying a lot think that they shouldn't be, and the people who aren't crying think that they should be. One man said to me that since he's not feeling anything when he does tonglen practice, maybe he should leave; he felt that he wasn't getting the point. He wasn't feeling mushy or warm; he was just kind of numb. I had to encourage him that a genuine experience of numbness is a genuine experience of what it is to be human.

It's all raw material for waking up. You can use numbness, mushiness, and self-pity even—it doesn't matter what it is—as long as you can go deeper, underneath the story line. That's where you connect with what it is to be human, and that's where the joy and well-being come from—from the sense of being real and seeing realness in others.

The slogan says that when the world is filled with evil, or when the world is filled with things that you just don't want, that can all be transformed into the path of awakening. Then there are various suggestions, such as "Drive all blames into one" and "Be grateful to everyone." A third suggestion is that you can transform seeming obstacles into awakening by flashing on the nonsolidity of things—on shunyata or absolute bodhichitta.

* * *

This slogan is quite a difficult one, and it's on this subject of shunyata: "Seeing confusion as the four kayas / Is unsurpassable shunyata protection." The part about seeing confusion is pretty accessible to all of us, but the rest of the slogan requires discussion.

The word *kaya* means body. The four kayas are *dharmakaya, sambhogakaya, nirmanakaya,* and *svabhavikakaya.* You could say that the four kayas are a way of describing how emptiness manifests and how we could experience it.

First there's a sense of the basic space of dharmakaya—dharma body. In our morning chants we say, "The essence of thoughts is dharmakaya; nothing whatever, but everything arises from it." Dharmakaya is the basic space from which everything arises, and everything that arises is essentially spacious—not fixed or clunky.

Sambhogakaya—the "enjoyment body"—points to the experience that space is not really emptiness as we know it; there's energy and color and movement. It's vibrant, like a rainbow or a bubble or the reflection of your face in a mirror. It's vivid, yet nonsubstantial at the same time. Sambhogakaya refers to this energetic quality, the fact that emptiness is fluid and vivid. Sound is often an image for sambhogakaya; you can't see or capture it, but it has vibration, energy, and movement.

Nirmanakaya—the third of the four kayas—

refers to the experience that emptiness manifests in form. Nirmanakaya is the means of communication with others. *The Heart Sutra* says, "Form is emptiness; emptiness is form." Nirmanakaya refers to the fact that phenomena actually manifest. Trees, grass, buildings, traffic, each of us, and the whole world actually manifest. That's the only way we can experience emptiness: appearance / emptiness, sound / emptiness. They're simultaneous. Whatever appears is vividly unreal in emptiness. Emptiness isn't really empty in the way we might think of it; it's vibrant and it manifests, yet usually all we see is the manifestation. We solidify it, we solidify ourselves, we solidify what we see. The whole thing becomes like a war or a seduction, and we are totally caught in the drama.

The fourth kaya is svabhavikakaya. Svabhavika-kaya means that the previous three arise at once; they're not really three separate things. The space, the energy, and the appearance arise together.

The slogan says, "Seeing confusion [the sense of obstacle, the things we don't want, the sense of interruption] as the four kayas / Is unsurpassable shunyata protection." Shunyata is protection because it cuts through the solidity of our thoughts, which are how we make everything—including ourselves—concrete and separate. It cuts through the way we're over here and everything else is over there.

As we know from some of the other slogans we've discussed, when confusion arises, it is part of the path. When confusion arises, it is juicy and rich. The sense of obstacle is very rich and can teach us. In these practices it's the necessary ingredient for being able to do tonglen or work with lojong at all. But this slogan is saying that when confusion arises not only do you practice tonglen and connect with the heart, but also you can flash on the nonsolidity of phenomena at any time. In other words, you can just drop it. We all know spontaneously what it feels like just to drop it. Out of the blue, you just drop it.

For instance, on a meditation retreat there are noodles for breakfast. Maybe in the beginning it seems funny, but halfway through breakfast you find yourself—instead of being mindful of the food, the chopsticks in your hand, the other people, and the good instructions you've received—talking to yourself about what a good breakfast would be, how you'd like to have a good breakfast like your mother used to make you in Brooklyn. It might be matzo ball soup or tortillas and beans or ham and eggs, but you want a good breakfast: burned bacon, like Mother used to make. You resent these noodles.

Then, not through any particular effort, you just drop it. To your surprise, there's a big world there. You see all these little lights glimmering in your empty lacquered bowl. You notice the sadness on someone's face. You realize that the man across from you is also thinking about breakfasts because he has a resentful look on his face, which makes you laugh because you were there just one second ago.

The world opens up and suddenly we're there for what's happening. The solidity of our thoughts becomes transparent, and we can connect automatically with this space—shunyata—in ourselves. We have the ability to drop our story line, to rouse ourselves.

That's an everyday experience of shunyata. But it's also a very advanced practice if you can do it when you don't happen to feel like it. If everything is solid and intense and you're wallowing in self-pity or something else, if someone says to you at that point, "Just drop it," even in the sweetest, kindest, most gentle voice, you want to punch the person in the nose. You just want to keep wallowing in resentment and self-pity.

The whole point of the practice of lojong is that you start where you are. The slogan "Abandon any hope of fruition" is also encouragement to just be where you are, with your numbness or resentment or whatever. Just start where you are. Then as a result of doing the practice, to your surprise you find that this week you can drop it more easily than last week; or this year you can drop it more easily than last year. As time goes by, you find that you can spontaneously just drop it more and more.

The same goes for compassion. We all have compassion. When we remember or see certain things, we can, without any effort at all, open our hearts. Then we're told to have compassion for our enemies, for the Juans of our life, for the people that we really hate. That's advanced practice. But as a result of doing lojong practice and giving up all hope of fruition, of just relating with who we are now and with what we're feeling now, we find that the circle of our compassion begins to widen, and we are able to feel compassion in increasingly difficult situations.

Compassion starts coming to us because we have the aspiration to do the practice and to get more in touch with our own pain and our own joy. In other words, we are willing to get real. We realize that we can't fake it and we can't force it, but we know we have what it takes to work with how we are right now. So we start that way, and both the ability to drop it and cheer up and the ability to open our hearts begin to grow of their own accord.

"Seeing confusion as the four kayas / Is unsurpassable shunyata protection" is really encouragement not to make such a big deal of things. We can at least entertain the thought that we could drop it and remember what it feels like when we do drop it—how the world opens up—and discover the big world outside of our little ego-bound cocoon.

This particular slogan is meant as meditation instruction. It's said that only on the cushion can you really get into this one. In general, however, I'd like to encourage you to use the whole lojong and tonglen approach as practice even after you finish your formal meditation period. That's where it's most powerful, most real, and most heartfelt. As you're going about your day and you're seeing things that touch your heart, or you're feeling things that scare you or make you feel uptight or resentful, you can begin to think of doing the exchange, breathing in and breathing out on the spot. This is necessary and helpful. After meditation this practice feels quite real, sometimes a lot more real than in the meditation room.

This slogan about the four kayas points out that it's in shamatha-vipashyana practice that you begin to see the nonsubstantial nature of things. It's addressed to that part of the practice where we say, "Thinking." You're completely caught up. You've gone to New York City in your mind, and you're having that breakfast, and you're reliving resentments and joys, and then without any effort, you wake up. That's what happens, as you know, but it's not like you make yourself come back. It's that suddenly you notice and wake up, and then you're told to say, "Thinking."

That label, "thinking," is the beginning of acknowledging that the whole drama doesn't have any substance, that it arises out of nowhere, but it seems extremely vivid. Even though the story line goes away, there's energy and movement. It definitely seems to manifest in terms of tables and chairs and people and animals, and it seems so tangible, but the moment you say, "Thinking," you're acknowledging that the whole drama is just a thought in your mind. That's a recognition of shunyata, or emptiness. Maybe each of us has had some moments of how liberating that can be.

When the thoughts arise it might occur to you to wonder where they come from. Where *do* they come from? It seems as if they come from nowhere. You're just faithfully following your breath and—Wham!—you're in Hawaii surfing. Where did it come from? And where does it *go*? Big drama, big drama's happening, big, big, drama. And it's 9:30 in the morning. "Oooh. Wow! This is extremely heavy." A car horn honks, and suddenly you're not in that drama anymore, you're in another drama.

I was once instructed to meditate on thoughts. I investigated the nature of thought for two whole months. I can tell you firsthand that you can never find a thought. There is nothing there of substance, but with our minds we make it Extremely Big Deal.

Another slogan says, "All activities should be done with one intention." Breathing in, breathing out, feeling resentful, feeling happy, being able to drop it, not being able to drop it, eating our food, brushing our teeth, walking, sitting—whatever we're doing could be done with one intention, which is that we want to wake up, we want to ripen our compassion, and we want to ripen our ability to let go. Everything in our lives can wake us up or put us to sleep, and basically it's up to us to let it wake us up.

11

Overcoming Resistance

THE SLOGAN of the day is "Four practices are the best of methods." This slogan is about the four things that help us to practice both relative and absolute bodhichitta: (1) accumulating merit, (2) purifying our negative actions—usually called confessing our negative actions, (3) feeding the ghosts, and (4) offering to the protectors, which is sometimes translated as asking the protectors to help you in your practice.

Each of these four practices jumps right into the guts of unwanted feelings, emotions, and situations. Earlier we talked about how the best kind of protection is to see the empty, dreamlike quality of the confusion. Whereas seeing confusion as the four kayas is something we do on the level of absolute bodhichitta, the four practices are about actual things that you can do at the relative level in terms of ritual and ceremony.

However you talk about it, the crux of the matter is to overcome resistance. These four practices are four methods that Milarepa might have used to try to get the demons out of his cave. The punch line of that story was that when the resistance was gone, so were the demons. Resistance to unwanted circumstances has the power to keep those circumstances alive and well for a very long time.

Accumulating merit. The first of the four practices is to accumulate merit. The way to accumulate merit is to be willing to give, willing to open, willing not to hold back. It is described as letting go of holding on to yourself, letting your stronghold of ego go. Instead of collecting things for yourself, you open and give them away.

As a result of opening yourself, you begin to experience your world as more friendly. That is merit. You find it easier to practice the dharma, you have fewer kleshas, and circumstances seem to be hospitable. You might think that the way to encounter circumstances in which you could practice the dharma is to use your same old habitual style. But the idea behind accumulating this kind of meritorious situation is to open, to give, and not to hold back. Instead of encasing yourself in a cocoon, instead of shielding your heart, you can open, let the whole thing dissolve. This is how merit is accumulated.

In Buddhist societies such as in Burma and Tibet and China, accumulating merit is interpreted as performing all kinds of good works, such as making donations to build monasteries or retreat centers. It's wonderful to fund-raise in Hong Kong and Taiwan because people feel that it's meritorious to give money to build a retreat center or a monastery. If you give to these worthy causes, and if it's a gesture of real generosity—if you're giving without wishing for anything particular in return—then it works.

When we take the bodhisattva vow, we give a gift. The moment we give the gift is the moment we receive one of the marks of taking the vow. The instruction is to give something that you find it hard to let go of, something that hurts a little. If you give money, it should be just a little more than you really wanted to give.

In all of these traditional ways of accumulating merit, the inner meaning is that of opening completely to the situation, with some kind of daring. There's an incantation that goes along with this, the practice of which is said to be the ultimate expression of gaining merit because it has to do with letting go of hope and fear: "If it's better for me to be sick, so be it. If it's better for me to recover, so be it. If it's better for me to die, so be it." Another way this is said is, "Grant your blessings that if I'm meant to be sick, let me be sick. Grant your blessings that if I'm meant to recover, let me recover." It's not that you're asking some higher power to grant the blessings; basically, you're just saying, "Let it happen, let it happen."

Surrendering, letting go of possessiveness, and complete nonattachment—all are synonyms for accumulating merit. The idea is to open up rather than shut down.

* * *

Confessing evil actions. The second of the four practices is to confess evil actions, or lay down neurotic
actions. In Buddhist monasteries, this is done cere-
monially on days of the full and new moons. Confessing your neurotic actions has four parts to it: (1)
regretting what you've done; (2) refraining from doing
it again; (3) performing some kind of remedial activity such as the Vajrasattva mantra, taking refuge in
the three jewels, or tonglen; and (4) expressing complete willingness to continue this fourfold process in
the future and not to act out neurotically. So the fourfold formula of laying down your neurosis consists of
regret, refraining, remedial action, and the resolve
not to do it again.

Bad circumstances may have arisen, but we know
that we can transform them. The advice here is that
one of the best methods is to confess the whole
thing. First, you don't confess to anybody; it's a personal matter. You yourself look at what you do and go
through this fourfold process with it. Second, no one
forgives you. You're not confessing sin; it's not as if
you've "sinned," as we were taught in the Judeo-
Christian culture in which we grew up.

What is meant by neurosis is that in limitless,
timeless space—with which we could connect at any
time—we continually have tunnel vision and lock
ourselves into a room and put bolts on the door.
When there's so much space, why do we keep put-

ting on dark glasses, putting in earplugs, and covering ourselves with armor?

Confessing our neurotic action is a fourfold process by which we learn to see honestly what we do and develop a yearning to take off those dark glasses, take out those earplugs, take off that armor and experience the world fully. It's yet again another method for letting go of holding back, another method for opening rather than closing down.

1. REGRET. So, first, regret. Because of mindfulness and seeing what you do, which is the result of your practice, it gets harder and harder to hide from yourself. Well, that turns out to be extremely good news, and it leads to being able to see neurosis as neurosis—not as a condemnation of yourself but as something that benefits you. Regret implies that you're tired of armoring yourself, tired of eating poison, tired of yelling at someone each time you feel threatened, tired of talking to yourself for hours each time you don't like the way someone else does something, tired of this constant complaint to yourself. Nobody else has to give you a hard time. Nobody has to tell you. Through keeping your eyes open, you yourself get tired of your neurosis. That's the idea of regret.

Once someone who had done something that he really regretted went to his teacher and explained the whole thing. The teacher said, "It's good that you feel that regret. You have to acknowledge what you do. It's much better that you see that you harmed somebody than that you protect yourself from that. But you only get two minutes for regret." That's a good thing to remember because otherwise you might flagellate yourself—"Oy vey, Oy vey."

2. REFRAINING. The second part of confessing neurotic action is refraining. It's painful when you see how in spite of everything you continue in your neurosis; sometimes it has to wear itself out like an old shoe. However, refraining is very helpful as long as you don't impose too authoritarian a voice on yourself. Refraining is not a New Year's resolution, not a setup where you plan your next failure by saying, "I see what I do and I will never do it again," and then you feel pretty bad when you do it again within the half hour.

Refraining comes about spontaneously when you see how your neurotic action works. You may say to yourself, "It would still feel good; it still looks like it would be fun," but you refrain because you already know the chain reaction of misery that it sets off. The initial bite, or the initial drink, or the initial harsh word might give you some feeling of well-being, but it's followed by the chain reaction of misery that you've been through not once but five thousand times. So refraining is a natural thing that comes from the fact that we have basic wisdom in us. It's important to remember that refraining is not harsh, like yelling at yourself or making yourself do something you don't want to do. It's gentle; at the very most, you say to yourself, "One day at a time."

3. REMEDIAL ACTION. The third part of confessing your neurotic activity is remedial action, doing something about the whole thing, doing some kind of practice to water the seed of wisdom, giving it the necessary moisture to grow. To see neurosis as neurosis, to have a sense of regret and to refrain, and then to do the practice helps to purify the whole situation. The practice traditionally suggested is to take refuge in the three jewels—the Buddha, the dharma, and the *sangha.*

To take refuge in the Buddha is to take refuge in someone who let go of holding back, just as you can do. To take refuge in the dharma is to take refuge in all the teachings that encourage you and nurture your inherent ability to let go of holding back. And to take refuge in the sangha is to take refuge in the community of people who share this longing to let go and open rather than shield themselves. The support that we give each other as practitioners is not the usual kind of samsaric support in which we all join the same team and complain about someone else. It's more that you're on your own, completely alone, but it's helpful to know that there are forty other people who are also going through this all by themselves. That's very supportive and encouraging. Fundamentally, even though other people can give you support, you do it yourself, and that's how you grow up in this process, rather than becoming more dependent.

4. RESOLUTION. The fourth aspect of laying down your evil action is the resolve not to repeat it. Again, this can be tricky if misunderstood: the point is not to be harsh with yourself. Don't let an authoritarian inner voice tell you that if you do it again you're going to get a lump of coal in the bottom of your stocking.

All four parts of this process come from confidence in your basic goodness. All four come out of some gentleness toward yourself because there's already a sense of appreciation. You can regret your neurosis and open. You can refrain from doing it again because you don't want to harm yourself anymore. You can practice because you have basic respect for yourself, and you wish to do what nurtures your sense of confidence and warriorship rather than what makes you feel more poverty-stricken and isolated. So, finally, resolving not to do it again becomes a complete surrender, the last stage in a fourfold process of opening further.

Feeding the ghosts. So far we've described two of the practices in "Four practices are the best of methods": accumulating merit and confessing our neurotic crimes, or purifying our neurosis through this fourfold process. The third practice is to feed the ghosts. This involves relating to your unreasonableness. The way you relate to it is by making a relationship with it. Traditionally, you make a little *torma*—a little cake—

and you offer it. Maybe you offer it during a ceremony, maybe you put it out each morning, but in any
case you physically offer something to the ghosts, the
negative aspects of yourself.

When Trungpa Rinpoche talked about feeding the
ghosts, he talked about unreasonableness that just
pops up out of nowhere. Out of nowhere we are un-
bearably sad. Out of nowhere we're furious and we
want to destroy the place. He said, "Your fists are at
your wife's eyes." What an image! Without a warning,
unreasonableness just comes up out of nowhere—
Bang!—there it is. Frequently it comes first thing in
the morning, and then the whole day has that angry,
pissed-off feeling. It's the same with sadness, the
same with passion.

This sudden unreasonableness that comes out of
nowhere is called a *dön*. It wakes you up, and you
should regard that as best, rather than try to get rid of
the problem. So, on the outer level, you give the dön
a cake. On the inner level, you see that a dön has
risen, that it has all this force, but you refrain from
blackening anybody's eyes, from acting it out, and
you also refrain from repressing it. You take the middle way yet again and let yourself be there with the
full force of the dön. Being there has the power to purify you. That's a description of 100 percent mindfulness.

Just as you accumulate merit by going beyond
hope and fear and saying, "Let it be," the same with

the dön; there's some sense of "let it be." There is even an incantation that says, "Not only do I not want you to go away, you can come back any time you like. And here, have some cake."

Personally, when I read that, I got sort of scared. The commentary said that you invite them back because they show you when you have lost your mindfulness. You invite them back because they remind you that you've spaced out. The döns wake you up. As long as you are mindful, no dön can arise. But they're like cold germs, viruses; wherever there's a gap—Boom!—in they come. The dön will refuse your invitation to come back as long as you're awake and open, but the moment you start closing off, it will accept your invitation with pleasure and eat your cake anytime. That's called feeding the ghosts.

Offering to the protectors. The fourth practice is to offer to the protectors, or ask the protectors to help you with your practice. The protectors protect the principle of enlightenment; they protect our inherent wisdom, our inherent compassion. In *thangkas*—Tibetan scroll paintings—they appear as wrathful figures with flames coming out of them, big teeth and claws, and necklaces of skulls. The protectors are protecting against unkindness, against lapses of wisdom, against harshness and petty-mindedness, against fundamental insanity of any kind. The reason they appear so wrathful is that they're not going to buy that stuff. And who is it that's not going to buy that stuff? In truth, it's your own wisdom.

Under this slogan comes the teaching on learning to appreciate the giant *No*. Again, this is based on respect for yourself, loving-kindness for yourself, which is to say, confidence in your basic goodness. When you start to close down and shut off, an abruptness occurs, which is basically the giant No. It is not authoritarian in the sense that somebody's out to punish you. It is inherent encouragement not to spin off into neurotic stuff.

When anger or any other klesha arises, its basic energy is powerful, clean, and sharp and can cut through any neurosis. But usually we don't stop at that. We usually spin off into what's been called negative negativity, which is pettiness, resentment, aggression, righteous indignation. Then this protector aspect of the mind that protects your basic wisdom rears its flame-covered head and says *No*. Learning to appreciate the giant No comes out of compassion for yourself and is very similar to regretting, refraining, taking refuge in the three jewels, and resolving not to do it again.

Let's say you're all upset, you're yelling at someone and they're yelling back, there's a big fight going on, you stomp out the door and slam it on your finger. That's the essence of the protector principle. It wakes you up.

The outer practice is to offer to the protectors,

the wisdom principle. Traditionally you offer cake. At the inner level, you're inviting that principle to be alive and well in your being. You're willing to practice in order to nurture your ability to know when you're awake and when you're falling asleep and to bring yourself back to the wakefulness of the present moment.

In the lojong teachings, the approach is that the best way to use unwanted circumstances on the path of enlightenment is not to resist but to lean into them. Befriending emotions or developing compassion for those embarrassing aspects of ourselves, the ones that we think of as sinful or bad, becomes the raw material, the juicy stuff with which we can work to awaken ourselves. The four practices are the best of methods for overcoming resistance, the best of methods for transforming bad circumstances into the way of enlightenment.

12

Empty Boat

I HAD AN INTERVIEW with someone who said she couldn't meditate; it was impossible because she had real-life problems. In the meditation we're doing we're trying to bring home the very supportive message that real-life problems are the material for waking up, not the reason to stop trying. This is news you can use.

Today's slogan is "Whatever you meet unexpectedly, join with meditation." This is a very interesting suggestion. These slogans are pointing out that we can awaken bodhichitta through everything, that nothing is an interruption. This slogan points out how interruptions themselves awaken us, how interruptions themselves—surprises, unexpected events, bolts out of the blue—can awaken us to the experience of both absolute and relative bodhichitta, to the open, spacious quality of our minds and the warmth of our hearts.

This is the slogan about surprises as gifts. These surprises can be pleasant or unpleasant; the main point is that they can stop our minds. You're walking along and a snowball hits you on the side of the head. It stops your mind.

The slogan "Rest in the nature of alaya, the essence" goes along with this. Usually it is considered a slogan for when you're sitting on the cushion meditating; you can then rest your mind in its natural, unbiased state. But the truth is that when the rug is pulled out the same thing happens: without any effort on our part, our mind finds itself resting in the nature of alaya.

I was being driven in a car one day, when a horn honked loudly from behind. A car comes up by my window and the driver's face is purple and he's shaking his fist at me—my window is rolled down and so is his—and he yells, "Get a job!" That one still stops my mind.

The instruction is that when something stops your mind, catch that moment of gap, that moment of big space, that moment of bewilderment, that moment of total astonishment, and let yourself rest in it a little longer than you ordinarily might.

Interestingly enough, this is also the instruction on how to die. The moment of death is apparently a major surprise. Perhaps you've heard this word *samadhi* (meditative absorption), that we remain in samadhi at the moment we die. What that means is that we can rest our minds in the nature of alaya. We can stay open and connect with the fresh, unbiased quality of our minds, which is given to us at the moment of our death. But it's also given to us throughout every day of our lives! This gift is given to us by the unexpected circumstances referred to in this slogan.

After the gap, when you've begun to talk to yourself again—"That horrible person" or "Wasn't that wonderful that he allowed me to rest my mind in the nature of alaya?"—you could catch yourself and start to do tonglen practice. If you're veering off toward anger, resentment, any of the more unwanted "negative" feelings, getting really uptight and so forth, you could remember tonglen and the lojong logic and breathe in and get in touch with your feeling. Let the story line go and get in touch. If you start talking to yourself about what a wonderful thing just happened, you could remember and send that out and share that sense of delight.

Usually we're so caught up in ourselves, we're hanging on to ourselves so tightly, that it takes a Mack truck knocking us down to wake us up and stop our minds. But really, as you begin to practice, it could just take the wind blowing the curtain. The surprise can be something very gentle, just a shift of attention. Something just catches your eye and your attention shifts, and you can rest your mind in the nature of alaya. When you start talking to yourself again, you can practice tonglen.

The surprise comes in pleasant and unpleasant forms—it doesn't really matter how. The point is that it comes out of the blue. You're walking down the street, caught in tunnel vision—talking to yourself—and not noticing anything, and even the croak of a raven can wake you up out of your daydream, which is often very thick, very resentful. Something just pops it; a car backfires, and for a moment you look up and see the sky and people's faces and traffic going by and the trees. Whatever is happening there, suddenly you see this big world outside of your tunnel vision.

I had an interesting experience of something surprising me like this on retreat. It was a very strong experience of shunyata, the complete emptiness of things. I had just finished my evening practice. I had been practicing all day, after which you might think I would be in a calm, saintly state of mind. But as I came out of my room and started to walk down the hall, I saw that in our serving area someone had left dirty dishes. I started to get really angry.

Now, in this retreat we put our name on our dishes. Everyone has a plate and a bowl and a mug and a knife and a fork and a spoon, and they all have our name on them. So I was walking down and I was trying to see whose name was on those dishes. I was already pretty sure whose name was on them, because there was only one woman of our group of eight who would leave such a mess. She was always just leaving things around for other people to clean up. Who did she think was going to wash these dishes, her mother? Did she think we were all her slaves? I was really getting into this. I was thinking, "I've known her for a long time, and everyone thinks she's a senior practitioner, but actually she might as well have never meditated for the way she's so inconsiderate of everybody else on this planet."

When I got to the sink, I looked at the plate, and the name on it was "Pema," and the name on the cup was "Pema," and the name on the fork was "Pema," and the name on the knife was "Pema." It was all mine! Needless to say, that cut my trip considerably. It also stopped my mind.

There's a Zen story in which a man is enjoying himself on a river at dusk. He sees another boat coming down the river toward him. At first it seems so nice to him that someone else is also enjoying the river on a nice summer evening. Then he realizes that the boat is coming right toward him, faster and faster. He begins to get upset and starts to yell, "Hey, hey, watch out! For Pete's sake, turn aside!" But the boat just comes faster and faster, right toward him. By this time he's standing up in his boat, screaming and shaking his fist, and then the boat smashes right into him. He sees that it's an empty boat.

This is the classic story of our whole life situation. There are a lot of empty boats out there that we're always screaming at and shaking our fists at. Instead, we could let them stop our minds. Even if they only stop our mind for one point one seconds, we can rest in that little gap. When the story line starts, we can do the tonglen practice of exchanging ourselves for others. In this way everything we meet has the potential to help us cultivate compassion and reconnect with the spacious, open quality of our minds.

13

Teachings for Life and Death

THE FIVE STRENGTHS are the subject of two of the slogans: "Practice the five strengths, / The condensed heart instructions" and "The mahayana instruction for ejection of consciousness at death / Is the five strengths: how you conduct yourself is important."

The underlying point of all our study and practice is that the happiness we seek is here to connect with at any time. The happiness we seek is our birthright. To discover it we need to be more gentle with ourselves, more compassionate toward ourselves and our universe. The happiness we seek cannot be found through grasping, trying to hold on to things. It cannot be found through getting serious and uptight about wanting things to go in the direction that we think will bring happiness. We are always taking hold of the wrong end of the stick. The point is that the happiness we seek is already here and it will be found through relaxation and letting go rather than through struggle.

Does that mean you can just sleep all day? Does that mean there's nothing you need to do? The answer is no. There does seem to be something that we have to do. These slogans tell us to practice the five strengths: strong determination, familiarization, seed of virtue, reproach, and aspiration. The five strengths are five sources of inspiration to trust that we've got all that we need in the palm of our hand.

These are the heart instructions on how to live and how to die. Last year I spent some time with two people who were dying. Jack and Jill were both old friends; they each had a very different relationship with their death. They each had the privilege of knowing quite a few months in advance that they were going to die, which is a great gift. Both of them began to fade away. When things began to slip away on Jack, when his body stopped working well for him, he was angry at the beginning, but then something started to shift, and he began to relax. When it was clear that everything was dissolving and slipping away, he seemed to get happier and happier. It felt as if he were letting go of all the things that had kept him separate from his basic goodness, letting everything go. He would say things like, "There's nothing to do, there's nothing to want," and he would start to laugh. Day by day he wasted away more, but that was not a fundamental problem; this dissolving was very liberating for him.

The external situation was the same for Jill, but she got scared, and she began to struggle against the whole process. As her body started to waste away and there was less to hold on to, she became more grim and terrified, clenching her teeth and her hands. She was facing a vast abyss and was going to be pushed over into it, and she was screaming with terror, "No! No! No!"

I understood why I practice: we can discover the process of letting go and relaxing during our lifetime. In fact, that's the way to live: stop struggling against the fact that things are slipping through our fingers. Stop struggling against the fact that nothing's solid to begin with and things don't last. Knowing that can give us a lot of space and a lot of room if we can relax with it instead of screaming and struggling against it.

The five strengths are instruction on how to live and how to die. Actually, there's no difference. The same good advice applies to both, because if you know how to die then you know how to live and if you know how to live then you'll know how to die. Suzuki Roshi said, "Just be willing to die over and over again." As each breath goes out, let it be the end of that moment and the birth of something new. All those thoughts, as they come up, just see them and let them go, let the whole story line die; let the space for something new arise. The five strengths address how to give up trying all the time to grasp what's un-graspable and actually relax into the space that's there. Then what do we find? Maybe that's the point. We're afraid to find out.

Strong determination. The first strength is strong determination. Rather than some kind of dogged pushing through, strong determination involves connecting with joy, relaxing, and trusting. It's determination to use every challenge you meet as an opportunity to open your heart and soften, determination not to withdraw. One simple way to develop this strength is to develop a strong-hearted spiritual appetite. To do this, some kind of playful quality is needed. When you wake up in the morning, you can say: "I wonder what's going to happen today. This may be the day that I die. This may be the day that I understand what all these teachings are about." The Native Americans, before they went into battle, would say, "Today is a good day to die." You could also say, "Today is a good day to live."

Strong determination gives you the vehicle that you need to find out for yourself that you have everything it takes, that the fundamental happiness is right here, waiting. Strong determination not to shut anything out of your heart and not to close up takes a sense of humor and an appetite, an appetite for enlightenment.

Familiarization. The next strength is familiarization. What familiarization means is that the dharma no longer feels like a foreign entity: your first thought becomes dharmic. You begin to realize that all the teachings are about yourself; you're here to study yourself. Dharma isn't philosophy. Dharma is basically a good recipe for how to cook yourself, how to soften the hardest, toughest piece of meat. Dharma is good instruction on how to stop cheating yourself, how to stop robbing yourself, how to find out who you really are, not in the limited sense of "I need" and "I'm gonna get," but through developing wakefulness as your habit, your way of perceiving everything.

We talk about enlightenment as if it's a big accomplishment. Basically, it has to do with relaxing and finding out what you already have. The enlightened "you" might be a slightly different "you" from the one you're familiar with, but it still has hair growing out of its head, still has taste buds, and when it gets the flu, snot comes out of its nose. Enlightened, however, you might experience yourself in a slightly less claustrophobic way, maybe a completely nonclaustrophobic way.

Familiarization means that you don't have to search any further, and you know it. It's all in the "pleasantness of the presentness," in the very discursive thoughts you're having now, in all the emotions that are coursing through you; it's all in there somehow.

Seed of virtue. The third strength is called the seed of virtue. In effect, this is buddha nature or basic goodness. It's like a swimming pool with no sides that you're swimming in forever. In fact, you're made out of water. Buddha nature isn't like a heart transplant that you get from elsewhere. "It isn't as if you're trying to teach a tree to talk," as Rinpoche once said. It's just something that can be awakened or, you might say, relaxed into. Let yourself fall apart into wakefulness. The strength comes from the fact that the seed is already there; with warmth and moisture it sprouts and becomes visible above the ground. You find yourself looking like a daffodil, or feeling like one, anyway. The practice is about softening or relaxing, but it's also about precision and seeing clearly. None of that implies searching. Searching for happiness prevents us from ever finding it.

Reproach. The fourth strength is called reproach. This one requires talking to yourself: "Ego, you've done nothing but cause me problems for ages. Give me a break. I'm not buying it anymore." Try it in the shower. You should talk to yourself all the time without embarrassment. When you see yourself starting to spin off in frivolity, say to yourself, "Begone, you troublemaker!"

This approach can be slightly problematic because we don't usually distinguish between who we think we are and our ego. The more gentleness that comes up, the more friendliness you feel for yourself, the more this dialogue is fruitful. But to the degree that you actually are hard on yourself, then this dialogue could just increase your self-criticism.

Over the years, with encouragement from wonderful teachers, I have found that, rather than blaming yourself or yelling at yourself, you can teach the dharma to yourself. Reproach doesn't have to be a negative reaction to your personal brand of insanity. But it does imply that you see insanity as insanity, neurosis as neurosis, spinning off as spinning off. At that point, you can teach the dharma to yourself.

This advice was given to me by Thrangu Rinpoche. I was having anxiety attacks, and he said that I should teach the dharma to myself, just good simple dharma. So now I say, "Pema, what do you really want? Do you want to shut down and close off, do you want to stay imprisoned? Or do you want to let yourself relax here, let yourself die? Here's your chance to actually realize something. Here's your chance not to be stuck. So what do you really want? Do you want always to be right or do you want to wake up?"

Reproach can be very powerful. You yourself teach yourself the dharma in your own words. You can teach yourself the four noble truths, you can teach yourself about taking refuge—*anything* that has to do with that moment when you're just about to re-create samsara as if you personally had invented it. Look ahead to the rest of your life and ask yourself what you want it to add up to.

Each time you're willing to see your thoughts as empty, let them go, and come back to your breath, you're sowing seeds of wakefulness, seeds of being able to see the nature of mind, and seeds of being able to rest in unconditional space. It doesn't matter that you can't do it every time. Just the willingness, the strong determination to do it, is sowing the seeds of virtue. You find that you can do it more spontaneously and naturally, without its being an effort. It begins with some sense of exertion and becomes your normal state. That's the seed of bodhichitta ripening. You find out who you really are.

Aspiration. The last strength, aspiration, is also a powerful tool. A heartfelt sense of aspiring cuts through negativity about yourself; it cuts through the heavy trips you lay on yourself. The notion of aspiration is simply that you voice your wishes for enlightenment. You say to yourself, for yourself, about yourself, and by yourself things like, "May my compassion for myself increase." You might be feeling completely hopeless, down on yourself, and you can voice your heartfelt aspiration: "May my sense of being obstructed decrease. May my experience of wakefulness increase. May I experience my fundamental wisdom. May I think of others before myself." Aspiration is much like prayer, except that there's nobody who hears you.

Aspiration, yet again, is to talk to yourself, to be an eccentric bodhisattva. It is a way to empower yourself. In fact, all five of these strengths are ways to empower yourself. Buddhism itself is all about empowering yourself, not about getting what you want.

The five strengths are the heart instructions on how to live and how to die. Whether it's right now or at the moment of your death, they tell you how to wake up to whatever is going on.

14

Loving-Kindness and Compassion

ALL DHARMA AGREES at one point. All the teachings and all the practices are about just one thing: if the way that we protect ourselves is strong, then suffering is really strong too. If the ego or the cocoon starts getting lighter, then suffering is lighter as well. Ego is like a really fat person trying to get through a very narrow door. If there's lots of ego, then we're always getting squeezed and poked and irritated by everything that comes along. When something comes along that doesn't squeeze and poke and irritate us, we grasp it for dear life and want it to last forever. Then we suffer more as a result of holding on to ourselves.

One might think that we're talking about ego as enemy, about ego as original sin. But this is a very different approach, a much softer approach. Rather than original *sin,* there's original *soft spot.* The messy stuff that we see in ourselves and that we perceive in the world as violence and cruelty and fear is not the result of some basic badness but of the fact that we have such a tender, vulnerable, warm heart of bodhichitta, which we instinctively protect so that nothing will touch it.

This is a life-affirming view; it starts from the point of basic goodness or basic good heart. The problem is that we continually grab the wrong end of the stick. All practice agrees that there's some fundamental pattern that we have in which we're always trying to avoid the unpleasantness and grasp the pleasantness. There seems to be a need to change the fundamental pattern of always protecting against anything touching our soft spot. Tonglen practice is about changing the basic pattern.

Earlier, I referred to ego as being a room where you just tried to get everything on your own terms. To get out of that room, you don't drive up in a big machine and smash the whole thing to pieces. Rather, at your own speed, starting where you are, you begin to open the door and the windows. It's a very gentle approach, one that acknowledges that you *can* gradually begin to open that door. You can also shut it as often as you need to—not with the desire to stay comfortable but with the intention ultimately to gather more courage, more sense of humor, more basic curiosity about how to open that door, until you just leave it open and invite all sentient beings as your guests, until you feel at home with no agenda and with groundlessness.

The main thing about this practice and about all practice—all dharmas agree at one point—is that you're the only one who knows what is opening and what is closing down; you're the only one who knows. The next slogan, "Of the two witnesses, hold the principal one," is saying that one witness is everybody else giving you their feedback and opinions (which is worth listening to; there's some truth in what people say), but the principal witness is yourself. You're the only one who knows when you're opening and when you're closing. You're the only one who knows when you're using things to protect yourself and keep your ego together and when you're opening and letting things fall apart, letting the world come as it is—working with it rather than struggling against it. You're the only one who knows.

There's a later slogan that says, "Don't make gods into demons." What it means is that you can take something good—tonglen practice and the lojong teachings, for example (that's the idea of "gods")—and turn it into a demon. You can just use anything to close your windows and doors.

You could do tonglen as one of my students once described to me. He said, "I do it, but I am very careful about the control button; I breathe in just enough so that it doesn't really hurt or penetrate, and I breathe out just enough to convince myself, you know, that I'm doing the practice. But basically, nothing ever changes." He was using tonglen just to smooth everything out and feel good. You can also use tonglen to feel like a hero: you're just breathing in and out all over the place but your motivation isn't to befriend and begin to penetrate those areas of yourself that you fear or reject. In fact, you hope the practice will just bolster your sense of confidence, bolster your sense of being in the right place at the right time, having chosen the right religion, and "I'm on the side of the good and all's right with the world." That doesn't help much. Maybe you've noticed that sometimes you feel like you're in a battle with reality and reality is always winning.

All of the teachings, and particularly the lojong teachings, are encouraging us, if we find ourselves struggling, to let that be a moment where we pause and wonder and begin to breathe in, trying to feel what's underneath the struggle. If we find ourselves complaining, it isn't that we have to say, "Oh, I'm bad because I'm struggling." It's not that it's a sin to complain. We're simply saying that the way to change the pattern is to begin to breathe in and connect with the heart, the soft spot that's under all that protecting.

Karma is a difficult subject, but one of the reasons you are encouraged to work with what happens to you rather than blame it on others is that what happens is somehow a karmic result of things that you have done before. This kind of teaching on karma can easily be misunderstood. People get into a heavy-duty sin and guilt trip, feeling that if things are going wrong, that means they did something bad and they're being punished. That's not the idea at all. The idea of karma is that you continually get the teachings that you need in order to open your heart. To the degree that you didn't understand in the past how to stop protecting your soft spot, how to stop armoring your heart, you're given this gift of teachings in the form of your life, to give you everything you need to learn how to open further.

I saw a cartoon that describes this. A head of iceberg lettuce is sitting in a garden saying, "Oh, no, how did I get in this vegetable garden again? I wanted to be a wildflower!" The caption reads, "Oscar is born again as a head of iceberg lettuce in order to overcome his fear of being eaten." One can think from a bigger perspective than this whole notion of reward and punishment. You could see your life as an adult education course. Some of the curriculum you like and some you don't like; some of what comes up you find workable, some you don't. That's the curriculum for attaining enlightenment. The question is, how do you work with it?

When you begin to touch your heart or let your heart be touched, you begin to discover that it's bottomless, that it doesn't have any resolution, that this heart is huge, vast, and limitless. You begin to discover how much warmth and gentleness is there, as well as how much space. Your world seems less solid, more roomy and spacious. The burden lightens. In the beginning it might feel like sadness or a shaky feeling, accompanied by a lot of fear, but your willingness to feel the fear, to make fear your companion, is growing. You're willing to get to know yourself at this deep level. After awhile this same feeling begins to turn into a longing to raze all the walls, a longing to be fully human and to live in your world without always having to shut down and close off when certain things come along. It begins to turn into a longing to be there for your friends when they're in trouble, to be of real help to this poor, aching planet. Curiously enough, along with this longing and this sadness and this tenderness, there's an immense sense of well-being, unconditional well-being, which doesn't have anything to do with pleasant or unpleasant, good or bad, hope or fear, disgrace or fame. It's something that simply comes to you when you feel that you can keep your heart open.

15

Lighten Up

THE NEXT TWO SLOGANS—"Always maintain only a joyful mind" and "If you can practice even when distracted, you are well trained"—go hand in hand. The first is saying that if you regard everything that arises as fuel to wake up, you can remain cheerful. The second is saying that you are well trained if you *can* do that—use everything in your life to wake yourself up rather than put yourself to sleep—no matter what.

If you feel completely caught up and are spinning off into a misery scenario, the slogan "If you can practice even when distracted, you are well trained" can remind you to start to work with tonglen—to breathe in the mishap or the misery as a way of developing compassion for yourself and as a way of beginning to understand other people's pain as well. You can use the distraction to bring yourself back to the present moment, just as a horse rights itself after losing balance or skiers catch themselves just as they are about to fall. Being well trained means you can catch yourself and come back to the present.

When things are going well, that can also be a reminder. Instead of habitually clinging to what's delightful, you could become accustomed to giving it away, sending it out to others on the outbreath. This enables you always to maintain a joyful mind. It begins to ease away the burden of maintaining your own private happiness as well as your usual load of unhappy situations and minor irritations—the burden of ego.

On the other hand, sending out the joyful stuff is also difficult to do. As someone said, "I like doing the outbreath with this idea of sharing. Sharing is really nice, but giving it away? That means I wouldn't have it anymore." The outbreath and sharing what's pleasant can be threatening. You don't often feel willing to share or give away that pleasure.

There's a lot of joy as your burden begins to lessen, and it comes from doing anything that begins to change the pattern of fearing and wanting to resist what's unpleasant. Resistance is really what causes the pain; more than the anger itself, or the jealousy itself, it's resistance that causes the pain. Anything that begins to lighten up that resistance helps us to relax and open and celebrate.

Sooner or later you will find yourself in a situation where you can't change the outer circumstances at all, and you realize it all comes down to how you relate to things—whether you continue to struggle against everything that's coming at you or you begin to work with things. "Always maintain only a joyful mind" can be very helpful to remember in such a situation.

Anything that helps us not to be so desperate about pleasure and not to fear its transitory nature is also introducing us to being at home in our world and being able to help other people. In popular songs you hear lines like "Freedom's just another word for nothing left to lose" or "I've got plenty of nothing and nothing's plenty for me." "Great bliss arising from the experience of emptiness" is how it's described in traditional Tibetan texts, which sounds somewhat remote from personal experience. However, all these words are saying the same thing: we practice and we live in order to be able to relax and lighten up and not make such a big deal about everything that happens—the successes and the failures, the rewards and the punishments.

If your principal witness (in "Of the two witnesses, hold the principal one") is a judgmental authority figure, it might be hard to lighten up. Let's say you're meditating, but there's this other "you" standing behind with a stick, saying, "You're thinking again, you're always thinking! Whack! There goes the tonglen bell and you didn't practice tonglen for even a second! Smack!" You say to yourself, "I can't do this. I'm hopeless. Everybody else seems to be doing fine, but I don't seem to have any basic goodness." Then you beat yourself up and forget all about gentleness, or if you remember, you say, "You're not gentle! Whack!"

You hear a slogan like "Always maintain only a joyful mind," and for the whole next two weeks you're just hitting yourself over the head for never being joyful. That kind of witness is a bit heavy. So lighten up. Don't make such a big deal. The key to feeling at home with your body, mind, and emotions, to feeling worthy to live on this planet, comes from being able to lighten up. This earnestness, this seriousness about everything in our lives—including practice— this goal-oriented, we're-going-to-do-it-or-else attitude, is the world's greatest killjoy. There's no sense of appreciation because we're so solemn about everything. In contrast, a joyful mind is very ordinary and relaxed.

Once on retreat I was reading some traditional text that talked about bliss and special experiences, and I began to feel wretched. I felt poverty-stricken about never having had any experiences that felt like bliss, clarity, or luminosity. I began to feel depressed that I didn't measure up to any of these glowing words. Fortunately, I put that book down and picked up something simple about just being alive with who you are right now—nothing special, no big deal, ordinary: just keep your eyes open, keep your ears open, stay awake. Those simple instructions began to cheer me up, because I felt that I could follow them.

When your aspiration is to lighten up, you begin to

have a sense of humor. Things just keep popping your serious state of mind. In addition to a sense of humor, a basic support for a joyful mind is curiosity, paying attention, taking an interest in the world around you. You don't actually have to be happy. But being curious without a heavy judgmental attitude helps. If you *are* judgmental, you can even be curious about that.

Notice everything. Appreciate everything, including the ordinary. That's how to click in with joyfulness or cheerfulness. Curiosity encourages cheering up. So does simply remembering to do something different. We are so locked into this sense of burden—Big Deal Joy and Big Deal Unhappiness—that it's sometimes helpful just to change the pattern. Anything out of the ordinary will help, and tonglen is definitely something different. This practice is about repatterning ourselves, changing the basic pattern and unpatterning ourselves together. You can also just go to the window and look at the sky. You can splash cold water on your face, you can sing in the shower, you can go jogging—anything that's against your usual pattern. That's how things start to lighten up.

I just read a story about a woman who had been gloomy all her life. As she grew older, she got more irritable and difficult. Then she got cancer and for some peculiar reason—after an initial period of resistance and anger—instead of getting more gloomy, she began to cheer up. The more she fell apart, the happier she got. She kept saying she was glad that she had this time to enjoy her life, which she had not enjoyed up to the moment that she got sick. Finally, the day before she died, she went into a coma. Everybody in her family, who were coming to feel more and more fond of her after all those years of finding her to be a pain in the neck, gathered around her bed crying and looking gloomy, just as she used to look. Just before she died, she opened her eyes to see them all standing there, and she said, "Gosh, you all look so unhappy. Is something wrong?" She died laughing.

So, "Always maintain only a joyful mind" and "If you can practice even when distracted, you are well trained" are implying that the best gift you can give yourself is to lighten up. One way to do that is to let distraction bring you back to the present moment. Another way is to be curious. In addition, when things are really heavy and you feel stuck in either your joy or your misery, just do something different to change the pattern. Tonglen is a good suggestion of what you could do.

16

Abandon Any Hope of Fruition

OUR NEXT SLOGAN is "Abandon any hope of fruition." You could also say, "Give up all hope" or "Give up" or just "Give." The shorter the better.

One of the most powerful teachings of the Buddhist tradition is that as long as you are wishing for things to change, they never will. As long as you're wanting yourself to get better, you won't. As long as you have an orientation toward the future, you can never just relax into what you already have or already are.

One of the deepest habitual patterns that we have is to feel that now is not good enough. We think back to the past a lot, which maybe was better than now, or perhaps worse. We also think ahead quite a bit to the future—which we may fear—always holding out hope that it might be a little bit better than now. Even if now is going really well—we have good health and we've met the person of our dreams, or we just had a child or got the job we wanted—nevertheless there's a deep tendency always to think about how it's going to be later. We don't quite give ourselves full credit for who we are in the present.

For example, it's easy to hope that things will improve as a result of meditation, that we won't have such bad tempers anymore or we won't have fear anymore or people will like us more than they do now. Or maybe none of those things are problems for us, but we feel we aren't spiritual enough. Surely we will connect with that awake, brilliant, sacred world that we are going to find through meditation. In everything we read—whether it's philosophy or dharma books or psychology—there's the implication that we're caught in some kind of very small perspective and that if we just did the right things, we'd begin to connect with a bigger world, a vaster world, different from the one we're in now.

One reason I wanted to talk about giving up all hope of fruition is because I've been meditating and giving dharma talks for some time now, but I find that I still have a secret passion for what it's going to be like when—as they say in some of the classical texts—"all the veils have been removed." It's that same feeling of wanting to jump over yourself and find something that's more awake than the present situation, more alert than the present situation. Sometimes this occurs at a very mundane level: you want to be thinner, have less acne or more hair. But somehow there's almost always a subtle or not so subtle sense of disappointment, a sense of things not completely measuring up.

In one of the first teachings I ever heard, the teacher said, "I don't know why you came here, but I want to tell you right now that the basis of this whole teaching is that you're never going to get everything together." I felt a little like he had just slapped me in the face or thrown cold water over my head. But I've always remembered it. He said, "You're never going to get it all together." There isn't going to be some precious future time when all the loose ends will be tied up. Even though it was shocking to me, it rang true. One of the things that keeps us unhappy is this continual searching for pleasure or security, searching for a little more comfortable situation, either at the domestic level or at the spiritual level or at the level of mental peace.

Nowadays, people go to a lot of different places trying to find what they're looking for. There are 12-step programs; someone told me that there is now a 24-step program; someday there will probably be a 108-step program. There are a lot of support groups and different therapies. Many people feel wounded and are looking for something to heal them. To me it seems that at the root of healing, at the root of feeling like a fully adult person, is the premise that you're not going to try to make anything go away, that what you have is worth appreciating. But this is hard to swallow if what you have is pain.

In Boston there's a stress-reduction clinic run on Buddhist principles. It was started by Dr. Jon Kabat-Zinn, a Buddhist practitioner and author of *Full Catastrophe Living*. He says that the basic premise of his clinic—to which many people come with a lot of pain—is to give up any hope of fruition. Otherwise the treatment won't work. If there's some sense of wanting to change yourself, then it comes from a place of feeling that you're not good enough. It comes from aggression toward yourself, dislike of your present mind, speech, or body; there's something about yourself that you feel is not good enough. People come to the clinic with addictions, abuse issues, or stress from work—with all kinds of issues. Yet this simple ingredient of giving up hope is the most important ingredient for developing sanity and healing.

That's the main thing. As long as you're wanting to be thinner, smarter, more enlightened, less uptight, or whatever it might be, somehow you're always going to be approaching your problem with the very same logic that created it to begin with: you're not good enough. That's why the habitual pattern never unwinds itself when you're trying to improve, because you go about it in exactly the same habitual style that caused all the pain to start.

There's a life-affirming teaching in Buddhism, which is that Buddha, which means "awake," is not someone you worship. Buddha is not someone you aspire to; Buddha is not somebody who was born more than two thousand years ago and was smarter than you'll ever be. Buddha is our inherent nature— our buddha nature—and what that means is that if you're going to grow up fully, the way that it happens is that you begin to connect with the intelligence that you already have. It's not like some intelligence that's going to be transplanted into you. If you're going to be fully mature, you will no longer be imprisoned in the childhood feeling that you always need to protect yourself or shield yourself because things are too harsh. If you're going to be a grown-up—which I would define as being completely at home in your world no matter how difficult the situation—it's because you will allow something that's already in you to be nurtured. You allow it to grow, you allow it to come out, instead of all the time shielding it and protecting it and keeping it buried.

Someone once told me, "When you feel afraid, that's 'fearful buddha.'" That could be applied to whatever you feel. Maybe anger is your thing. You just go out of control and you see red, and the next thing you know you're yelling or throwing something or hitting someone. At that time, begin to accept the fact that that's "enraged buddha." If you feel jealous, that's "jealous buddha." If you have indigestion, that's "buddha with heartburn." If you're happy, "happy buddha"; if bored, "bored buddha." In other words, anything that you can experience or think is worthy of compassion; anything you could think or feel is worthy of appreciation.

This teaching was powerful for me; it stuck. I would find myself in various states of mind and various moods, going up and down, going left and right, falling on my face and sitting up—just in all these different life situations—and I would remember, "Buddha falling flat on her face; buddha feeling on top of the world; buddha longing for yesterday." I began to learn that I couldn't get away from buddha no matter how hard I tried. I could stick with myself through thick and thin. If one would enter into an unconditional relationship with oneself, one would be entering into an unconditional relationship with buddha.

This is why the slogan says, "Abandon any hope of fruition." "Fruition" implies that at a future time you will feel good. There is another word, which is *open*—to have an open heart and open mind. This is oriented very much to the present. If you enter into an unconditional relationship with yourself, that means sticking with the buddha right now on the spot as you find yourself.

Because it's a monastery, there's nothing you can do at Gampo Abbey that's fun, unless you like to meditate all the time or take walks in nature, but everything gets boring after awhile. There's no sex there, you can't drink there, you also can't lie. Occasionally we'll see a video, but that's rare and usually there's a dispute about what it's going to be. The food is sometimes good and sometimes terrible; it's just a very uncomfortable place. The reason it's uncomfortable is that you can't get away from yourself there. However, the more people make friends with themselves, the more they find it a nurturing and supportive place where you can find out the buddhaness of your own self as you are right now, today. Right now today, could you make an unconditional relationship with yourself? Just at the height you are, the weight you are, the amount of intelligence that you have, the burden of pain that you have? Could you enter into an unconditional relationship with that?

Giving up any hope of fruition has something in common with the title of my previous book, *The Wisdom of No Escape*. "No escape" leaves you continually right in the present, and the present is whatever it is, whatever mood you happen to be in, whatever thoughts you happen to be having. That's it.

Whether you get meditation instruction from the Theravada tradition or the Zen tradition or the Vajrayana tradition, the basic instruction is always about being awake in the present moment. What they don't tell you is that the present moment can be you, this you about whom you sometimes don't feel very good. That's what there is to wake up to.

When one of the emperors of China asked Bodhidharma (the Zen master who brought Zen from India to China) what enlightenment was, his answer was, "Lots of space, nothing holy." Meditation is nothing holy. Therefore there's nothing that you think or feel that somehow gets put in the category of "sin." There's nothing that you can think or feel that gets put in the category of "bad." There's nothing that you can think or feel that gets put in the category of "wrong." It's all good juicy stuff—the manure of waking up, the manure of achieving enlightenment, the art of living in the present moment.

17

Compassionate Action

HOW DO WE HELP? How do we create a saner world or a saner domestic situation or job situation, wherever we may be? How do we work with our actions and our speech and our minds in a way that opens up the space rather than closes it down? In other words, how do we create space for other people and ourselves to connect with our own wisdom? How do we create a space where we can find out how to become more a part of this world we are living in and less separate and isolated and afraid? How do we do that?

It all starts with loving-kindness for oneself, which in turn becomes loving-kindness for others. As the barriers come down around our own hearts, we are less afraid of other people. We are more able to hear what is being said, see what is in front of our eyes, and work in accord with what happens rather than struggle against it. The lojong teachings say that the way to help, the way to act compassionately, is to exchange oneself for other. When you can put yourself in someone else's shoes, then you know what is needed, and what would speak to the heart.

I recently received a letter from a friend in which

144

she dumped all over me and told me off. My first re-action was to be hurt and my second reaction was to get mad, and then I began to compose this letter in my mind, this very dharmic letter that I was going to write back to her using all the teachings and all the lojong logic to tell her off. Because of the style of our relationship, she would have been intimidated by a dharmic letter, but it wouldn't have helped anything. It would have further forced us into these roles of being two separate people, each of us believing in our roles more and more seriously, that I was the one who knew it all and she was the poor student. But on that day when I had spent so much energy composing this letter, just by a turn of circumstance, something happened to me that caused me to feel tremendous lone-liness. I felt sad and vulnerable. In that state of mind, I suddenly knew where my friend's letter had come from—loneliness and feeling left out. It was her at-tempt to communicate.

Sometimes when you're feeling miserable, you challenge people to see if they will still like you when you show them how ugly you can get. Because of how I myself was feeling I knew that what she needed was not for somebody to dump back on her. So I wrote a very different letter from what I had planned, an ex-tremely honest one that said, "You know, you can dump on me all you like and put all of your stuff out there, but I'm not going to give up on you." It wasn't a wishy-washy letter that avoided the issue that there had been a confrontation and that I had been hurt by it. On the other hand, it wasn't a letter in which I went to the other extreme and lashed out. For the first time, I felt I had experienced what it meant to exchange oneself for other. When you've been there you know what it feels like, and therefore you can give something that you know will open up the space and cause things to keep flowing. You can give something that will help someone else connect with their own insight and courage and gentleness, rather than further polarize the situation.

"Drive all blames into one" is a pivotal slogan because usually driving blames into *other* comes from the fact that we've been hurt and therefore want to hurt back. It's that kind of logic. Therefore the exchange—putting ourselves in someone else's shoes—doesn't come from theory, in which you try to imagine what someone else is feeling. It comes from becoming so familiar and so openhearted and so honest about who you are and what you do that you begin to understand humanness altogether and you can speak appropriately to the situation.

The basic ground of compassionate action is the importance of working *with* rather than struggling *against,* and what I mean by that is working with your own unwanted, unacceptable stuff, so that when the unacceptable and unwanted appears out *there,* you relate to it based on having worked with loving-kindness for yourself. Then there is no condescension.

This nondualistic approach is true to the heart because it's based on our kinship with each other. We know what to say, because we have experienced closing down, shutting off, being angry, hurt, rebellious, and so forth, and have made a relationship with those things in ourselves.

This is not about problem resolution. This is a more open-ended and courageous approach. It has to do with not knowing what will happen. It has nothing to do with wanting to get ground under your feet. It's about keeping your heart and your mind open to whatever arises, without hope of fruition. Problem solving is based first on thinking there is a problem and second on thinking there is a solution. The concepts of problem and solution can keep us stuck in thinking that there is an enemy and a saint or a right way and a wrong way. The approach we're suggesting is more groundless than that.

A key slogan is "Change your attitude, but remain natural" or "Change your attitude and relax as it is."

In order to have compassionate relationships, compassionate communication, and compassionate social action, there has to be a fundamental change of attitude. The notion "I am the helper and you are the one who needs help" might work in a temporary way, but fundamentally nothing changes, because there's still one who has it and one who doesn't. That dualistic notion is not really speaking to the heart.

As expressed in the lojong teachings, that fundamental change of attitude is to breathe the undesirable in and breathe the desirable out. In contrast, the attitude that is epidemic on the planet is that if it's unpleasant we push it away and if it's pleasant we hold tight and grasp it.

This change in attitude doesn't happen overnight; it happens gradually, at our own speed. If we have the aspiration to stop resisting those parts of ourselves that we find unacceptable and instead begin to breathe them in, this gives us much more space. We come to know every part of ourselves, with no more monsters in the closet, no more demons in the cave. We have some sense of turning on the lights and looking at ourselves honestly and with great compassion.

We could begin to get the hang of changing our attitude on an everyday level: when things are delightful and wonderful we give our pleasure away on the outbreath, sharing it with others. That also allows for enormous space—not just for us, but for everyone. When we do this, all of our inner obstacles that keep us from connecting with our inherent freshness and openness begin to dissolve. This is the fundamental change of attitude—this working with pain and pleasure in a revolutionary and courageous way.

When we work with pain by leaning into it and with pleasure by giving it away, it doesn't mean that we "grin and bear it." This approach is a lot more playful than that—like dancing with it. We realize that this separateness that we feel is a funny kind of mistake. We see that things were not dualistic from the start; we can wake up to that realization. The basis of any real kind of compassionate action is the insight that the others who seem to be out there are some kind of mirror image of ourselves. By making friends with yourself, you make friends with others. By hurting others, you hurt yourself.

Another slogan says, "Always abide by the three basic principles." The first basic principle is always to abide by any vows you have taken—the refuge vows that you take to become a Buddhist and the bodhisattva vows taken later as an expression of your wish to benefit others. The second principle is to refrain from showing off, or from outrageous conduct. The third is always to cultivate patience. So these are the three basic principles: keeping the vows you have taken, refraining from outrageous conduct, and cultivating patience.

Keeping the vows you have taken. The first principle, to keep the vows you have taken, speaks specifically to those of us who have taken the refuge vows and bodhisattva vows, but it may be helpful for everyone to hear a little bit about these vows. The refuge vow is basically about making a commitment to become a refugee, which in essence means that rather than always trying to get security, you begin to develop an attitude of wanting to step into uncharted territory. It's a vow that you take because you feel that the way to health and becoming a complete human being is to no longer hold so tightly to yourself. You long to go beyond that situation. You are no longer afraid of yourself. You can become a refugee because when you aren't afraid of yourself, you don't feel that you need a protected place to hide in.

The image of the bodhisattva vow could be, "Not afraid of others." When you take the bodhisattva vow you open the windows and doors and invite all sentient beings as your guests. Having understood the futility and pain of always holding on to yourself, you want to take the next step and begin to work with others.

You might think that you are working with others because you are much more sane than they are and you want to spread that sanity. But a more profound insight is that you realize that the only way to go further is to open those doors and windows and not protect yourself any more but work with whatever arrives. That's the only way to wake up further. The motivation for making friends with yourself becomes wanting to help others; these two work together. You know you can't help others if you're not making friends with yourself.

* * *

Refraining from outrageous conduct. The second basic principle is to refrain from outrageous conduct. If you have this ideal of yourself as a hero or helper or doctor and everybody else as the victim, the patient, the deprived, the underdog, you are continuing to create the notion of separateness. Someone might end up getting more food or better housing, and that's a big help; those things are necessary. But the fundamental problem of isolation, hatred, and aggression is not addressed. Or perhaps you get flamboyant in your helper role. You often see this with political action. People make a big display, and suddenly the whole thing doesn't have to do with helping anyone at all but with building themselves up.

In the seventies there was a famous photograph in which the National Guard were all lined up with their guns at an antiwar rally. A young woman had walked up and put a flower in the end of one of the guns, and the photo appeared in all the newspapers. I read a report in which the soldier who had been holding that gun—who later became a strong peace activist—said that he had never before experienced anything as aggressive as that young woman coming with her flower and smiling at everybody and making this big display. Most of those young guys in the National Guard were already questioning how they got on that particular side of the fence anyway. And then along came this flower child. She never looked in his eyes; she never had any sense of him as a person. It was all for display, and it hurt. So that's part of the point of this slogan. You have to question what's behind your action, especially if it is making a big splash.

Cultivating patience. The last of the three basic principles is to cultivate patience, which is the same as cultivating nonaggression. Patience and nonaggression are basically encouragement to wait. Sometimes I think of tonglen that way. You are in a situation in which you would normally just yell back or throw something or think of the person you are with in the same old stuck way. Instead it occurs to you to begin to do the exchange for other. This whole solid sense of self and other begins to get addressed when you cultivate patience. You learn to pause, learn to wait, learn to listen, and learn to look, allowing yourself and others some space—just slowing down the camera instead of speeding it up.

It's a little bit like the old advice to count to ten before you say something; it makes you pause. If you become afraid or angry, there is a natural kind of adrenalin principle, when the camera actually starts to speed up. The speeding up itself can bring you back to the present. You can use it as a reminder just to slow down and listen and look and wait and develop patience.

* * *

"Abandon poisonous food" and "Don't make gods into demons" are warnings that only you know whether what you are doing is good practice ("gods" or "good food"). Anything could be used to build yourself up and smooth things over and calm things down or to keep everything under control. Good food becomes poisonous food and gods become demons when you use them to keep yourself in that room with the doors and windows closed.

Another slogan that concerns compassionate action is "Work with the greatest defilements first." Developing loving-kindness for yourself is the basis for compassionate communication and relationship. The time is now, not later. The greatest defilement is what you consider to be the greatest obstacle. This slogan is suggesting that you start where you feel most stuck. Making friends with that will begin to automatically take care of the smaller obstacles.

Because the larger obstacles like rage or jealousy or terror are so dramatic, their vividness itself may be a reminder to work with the practice of tonglen. We may so take for granted the multitude of minor daily irritations that we don't even think of them as something to work with. To some degree they are the hardest obstacles to work with because they don't reveal themselves. The only way you know that these are arising is that you feel righteous indignation. Let righteous indignation be your guide that someone is holding on to themselves, and that someone is probably you.

If you begin to work with the greater defilements, or the major stuck places, these little ones tend to become more obvious to you as well. Whereas if you try to work with all of these little ones, they are like your hands and your nose; you don't even think of them as anything but you, and there is no sense of them as obstacle. You just buy them every time they happen.

Our greatest obstacles are also our greatest wisdom. In all the unwanted stuff there is something sharp and penetrating; there's great wisdom there. Suppose anger or rage is what we consider our greatest obstacle, or maybe it's addiction and craving. This breeds all kinds of conflict and tension and stress, but at the same time it has a penetrating quality that cuts through all of the confusion and delusion. It's both things at once.

When you realize that your greatest defilement is facing you and there seems no way to get out of it because it's so big, the instruction is, let go of the story line, let go of the conversation, and own your feeling completely. Let the words go and return to the essential quality of the underlying stuff. That's the notion of the inbreath, the notion of making friends with ourselves at a profound level. In the process we are making friends with all sentient beings, because that is what life is made of. Working with the greater defilements first is saying that now is the time, and also that our greatest obstacles are our greatest wealth. From the point of view of wanting to stay cozy and separate in your room, this work is extremely threatening. Part of the path of compassionate action is to begin to explore that notion of the inbreath and test it, to see if it rings true for you.

18

Taking Responsibility for Your Own Actions

W HAT REALLY HELPS another person, anyway? What really causes things to evolve in some kind of natural spontaneous way? The next slogans provide some direction. Each begins with the word *don't*. I like to call them the "naked truth" slogans.

Taking responsibility for your own actions is another way of talking about awakening bodhichitta, because part of taking responsibility is the quality of being able to see things very clearly. Another part of taking responsibility is gentleness, which goes along with not judging, not calling things right or wrong, good or bad, but looking gently and honestly at yourself. Finally there is also the ability to keep going forward. It's been described before as letting go, but in some sense at a personal level it's that you can just keep on going; you don't get completely overwhelmed by this identity as a loser or a winner, the abuser or the abused, the good guy or the bad guy. You just see what you do as clearly and as compassionately as you can and then go on. The next moment is always fresh and open. You don't have to get frozen in an identity of any kind.

A Gary Larson cartoon shows two Martians who are hiding behind a rock. They've set up a mirror on one side of the path in front of the rock, down which are walking a man and a woman. One Martian says to the other: "Let's see if it attacks its own image."

It seems that we do attack our own image continually, and usually that image appears to be be "out there." We want to blame men or we want to blame women or we want to blame white people or black people, or we want to blame politicians or the police; we want to blame *somebody.* There's some tendency to always put it out there, even if "out there" is our own body. Instead of working *with,* there is the tendency to struggle *against.* As a result, we become alienated. Then we take the wrong medicine for our illness by armoring ourselves in all these different ways, somehow not getting back to the soft spot.

So today's slogans present the great exposé. The first one is "Don't talk about injured limbs." In other words, don't talk about other people's defects. We all get the same kind of satisfaction when we are all sitting around the table discussing Mortimer's bad breath. Not only that, he has dandruff, and not only that, he laughs funny; not only that, he's stupid. There is this peculiar security we get out of talking about other people's defects. Sometimes we sugar-coat it and pretend that we're not really doing it. We say something like, "Hi there. Did you know that Juanita steals?" Then we say, "Oh no, I shouldn't have said that. Excuse me, that was really unkind for me to say that, and I won't say any more." We'd love to go on and on, but instead we say just enough to get people against Juanita but not enough for them to disapprove of us for slandering her.

Then there's "Don't ponder others." It's talking about putting down other people to build yourself up. Maybe you only do it mentally. After all, you don't actually say these things out loud, because people would disapprove, but in your mind you talk a lot about Mortimer: how you hate how he dresses and how he walks and how he stares coldly at you when you try to smile. You say, "Now this is enough. I've been criticizing Mortimer since the day I arrived here. I'm going to try to make friends," but Mortimer just meets your sunny false smile with an icy stare. So you continue to ponder Mortimer's awful ways as you sit here on the cushion, and you very seldom label it "thinking" or breathe it in. It doesn't occur to you to exchange yourself for Mortimer, and you certainly don't feel grateful to him.

The next is "Don't be so predictable," which has also been translated as, "Don't be so trustworthy." It's an interesting one. It's getting at how predictable we are, as everybody in the advertising world knows. They know exactly what to put on those billboards and those ads to make us want to buy their products. Even intelligent people like ourselves are sometimes magnetized by this propaganda because we're so predictable.

Particularly, we are 100 percent predictable in that if we don't like something we'll run the other way, and if we do like it we'll spend quite a lot of time and effort trying to somehow eat it whole. If someone does something nice for you, you always remember it and you want to repay their kindness. But if somebody hurts you, you remember it for the rest of your life and you always want to get revenge in one way or another. That's the meaning of this slogan "Don't be so predictable." Don't always react so predictably to pleasure and pain. Don't keep taking the wrong medicine for the illness.

The next one is very easy to understand: "Don't malign others." We put a lot of energy and time into gossiping about others. Perhaps there's somebody, maybe it's just one person, that you have a problem with. Maybe it's Pearl, who is so pitiful. She is always feeling left out, and you find yourself reminded of your mother, who's also like that. Somehow Pearl and your mother become all mixed up together, and you find yourself continually irritated and disgusted by the pitifulness of Pearl, and it keeps triggering a lot of stuff in you. Yet you don't have the slightest interest in actually getting to know Pearl and finding out what's going on there. You have no desire to communicate with Pearl and find out who she is. Instead there's some kind of satisfaction that you get from not liking her, and you spend a lot of time and energy talking to yourself about Pitiful Pearl, or whoever it might be—Horrible Horatio or Miserable Mortimer.

The next one is "Don't wait in ambush," yet another "naked truth" slogan. You have been taught that you should be a nice person; on the other hand, you don't feel so nice. Maybe you know something about your husband that he doesn't know you know. You keep it up your sleeve, waiting for just the right moment to spring it on him. One day you're in the middle of a big argument, very heated. He has just insulted you royally. At that moment you bring the ace down from your sleeve and really let him have it. That's called waiting in ambush. You are willing to be very patient until just the right moment comes along, and then you let someone have it. This isn't the path of the warrior, it's the path of the coward. Not only do you want to "win"; you aren't even willing to communicate. The aspiration to communicate with another person—to be able to listen and to speak from the heart—is what changes our old stuck patterns.

* * *

The next slogan, "Don't bring things to a painful point," in some way is saying the same thing. These are nuances of the human tragedy, nuances of the tragicomic situation in which we find ourselves. "Don't bring things to a painful point" is again saying, "Don't humiliate people." We do all of these things because we feel pain, because we feel hurt and separate. Instead of first making friends with what we're feeling and then, second, trying to communicate, we have all these ways of keeping the "us and them" story solid and strong. That's what causes all the pain on this earth, including the fact that the ecosystem is turned upside down. All of that comes from people not making friends with themselves and never being willing to communicate with the one they consider to be the troublemaker. That's how we stay caught in this battleground, this war zone.

The next slogan is "Don't transfer the ox's load to the cow." Let's say you're Juan's boss. When something comes along that you find unpleasant and don't want to do, you pass it on to Juan. You pass the burden to someone else. It's like that Greek myth about Atlas. He was just walking along innocently and somebody said, "Oh, Atlas, would you mind for a moment just holding the earth?"

We do that. When we don't like it, it doesn't occur to us to actually work with that feeling and communicate with the person who is asking us to do this, to somehow open up the situation and work in an honest, fearless way with what's going on. Instead we just give our burden to somebody else and ask *them* to hold it. It's called passing the buck.

The next slogan is "Don't act with a twist." It means don't be devious, but it's similar to those slogans about not eating poisonous food or turning gods into demons. You're willing to drive all blames into yourself very publicly so everyone will notice, because you want people to think well of you. Your motivation is to get others to think that you're a great person, which is the "twist." Or there's a person who's doing you wrong, and you remember lojong, but there's a twist. You don't say, "Buzz off, Juanita," or anything harsh. You're this sweet person who wins everyone's admiration, but the other side of this is that they dislike Juanita more and more for mistreating you. It's as if you set Juanita up by acting like a saint. That's the idea of acting with a twist. There are all kinds of ways to get sweet revenge.

Finally, "Don't seek others' pain as the limbs of your own happiness," which is to say, "Don't seek others' pain as a way to get happiness for yourself." We are glad when the troublemakers in our lives get hit by a truck or go bankrupt, or anything of that nature. I have a few people in my life who fall into this category, and I'm amazed at how happy I am when one of them writes me a letter and tells me that things are going badly. Conversely, I feel haunted by distaste when I hear that things are going well for them. There's still the memory of how they hurt me, and I wish they would just continue to go downhill and drop dead, painfully. That's how we seek others' pain as the limbs of our own happiness.

These slogans are a curious study of the human species. They reveal that we need to be very honest about what we do. Through seeing these things we can begin to have a lot of compassion, because in studying ourselves we're studying the whole human race. The monastic rules give us insight into what all these saintly monks and nuns were like at the time of the Buddha. There are rules like Don't cover your meat with rice so that the server will give you more meat, thinking that you don't have any. Don't irritate your roommate on purpose to get the person to leave so that you'll have the room to yourself. These are actually rules, the code for the monks and nuns coming from the time of the Buddha.

All the cartoons in the world and all the funny movies are made out of what this particular group of slogans is saying. When we are doing things like this, either we don't see it or we do see it and feel as if we've committed a sin, so we either zone out or make a big deal: "I malign others. I'm not fit to live on this earth. What a burden. The more I know myself, the more I see. I'm just continually gossiping. There's no hope for me. Oy vey." However, we can also just see what we do—not only with honesty but also with a sense of humor—and then keep going and not make a whole identity out of it.

However, we're still left with a question: when I feel my worst—when I feel jealous or like I need to get revenge—how do I give my best? The first step is to dive into the experience of feeling bad. Make friends with that feeling. The next step is to learn to communicate with the people that you feel are causing your pain and misery—not to learn how to prove them wrong and yourself right but how to communicate from the heart. This is a lifetime's journey, and a profound one; it's not something that happens quickly or easily.

19

Communication from the Heart

L ET'S CONTINUE with the exploration of compassionate action. We have a strong tendency to
distance ourselves from our experience because it
hurts, but the dharma provides encouragement to
move closer to that experience. Although there are
lots of words that could be used to explain compassionate action, I'd like to stress one word, and that
word is *communication*—in particular, communication from the heart.

"All activities should be done with one intention."
This one intention is to awaken bodhichitta, to
awaken the heart. We could say, "All activities should
be done with the intention of communicating." This
is a practical suggestion: all activities should be done
with the intention of speaking so that another person
can hear you, rather than using words that cause the
barriers to go up and the ears to close. In this process
we also learn how to listen and how to look.

* * *

There is an extremely pointed slogan that goes along with "All activities should be done with one intention": "Always meditate on whatever provokes resentment." Instead of the resentment being an obstacle, it's a reminder. Feeling irritated, restless, afraid, and hopeless is a reminder to listen more carefully. It's a reminder to stop talking; watch and listen. It's a reminder to use tonglen practice to allow some space.

For example, you hate this person who is standing in front of you. You just wanted to help a hungry person get food, and then you find yourself talking to the enemy—a bureaucrat, a politician, *them.* All you do is get more and more angry at them, so nothing happens. They grow more stubborn as you grow more furious and polarized and the sense of huge *me* versus huge *them* increases.

When we feel resentment, the words that we speak, the actions that we perform, and the thoughts that we have aren't going to produce the results that we're hoping for. Beyond that, we're so aggressive that we're not exactly adding any peace and harmony to the world. Resentment becomes a reminder not to feel bad about ourselves but to open further to the pain and to the awkwardness.

If we really want to communicate, we have to give up knowing what to do. When we come in with our agendas, they only block us from seeing the person in front of us. It's best to drop our five-year plans and accept the awkward sinking feeling that we are entering a situation naked. We don't know what will happen next or what we'll do.

The slogan "Keep the three inseparable" is saying that your actions, your speech, and your thoughts should be inseparable from this yearning to communicate from the heart. Everything you say can further polarize the situation and convince you of how separate you are. On the other hand, everything you say and do and think can support your desire to communicate, to move closer and step out of this myth of isolation and separateness that you're caught in.

Usually when we feel wronged, our only intention is to get revenge. The slogan "Correct all wrongs with one intention" is trying to cheer us up a bit, lighten up the situation, and add some space. The "one intention" is to exchange oneself for other. This is the key. To correct all wrongs with one intention is to hear what's being said, to see the person who is in front of you, and to be able to rest in not knowing what to say or how to act but just to watch and wait. Then out of your mouth comes something, because the person in front of you is saying, "Well, what do you think?" or "I don't know, see if you can convince me to do it your way," or they're just yelling at you.

If simply to learn how to communicate were our

life's challenge, not only might we be able to help find food for people who are hungry and shelter for people who are homeless, but we might even see a fundamental change—less aggression on the planet and more cooperation.

We *are* different; we are very different from each other. One person's idea of what is polite is someone else's idea of what is rude. In some cultures it's considered rude to belch when you're eating, and in others it shows that you enjoyed your meal. What might smell repulsive to one person might smell wonderful to another. We are really different, and we have to acknowledge that. But instead of going to war because of our differences, let's play soccer. It will be a strange game, given our instruction to let others have the victory and keep the defeat to ourselves, but that doesn't mean that we play to lose; it means that we play to *play.* We could play *together,* even though we're on opposite teams. There are no big stakes, just playing. There are different teams; otherwise the game won't work. But it doesn't have to lead to World War III or the destruction of the planet.

One of my favorite dharma teachers is Dr. Seuss; he captures the human condition so beautifully. One of his stories starts with two people walking toward each other along a narrow road. When they meet, they each refuse to step to the side so that the other can pass. Everyone else builds bridges and even whole cities around them, and life just goes on. But the two stubborn ones stand there for the rest of time, refusing to budge. It never occurs to them even after eighty-five years that they could be curious about why the other is refusing to move, or that they could try to communicate. They could have had a really interesting debate in all those years even if they had still never moved.

The point is not that you're trying to achieve harmony or smooth everything out. Good luck, if that's your goal. The point is to live together on this earth with our differences, to communicate for its own sake. The process is the main thing, not the fruition. If you achieve your goal with aggressive tactics, nothing really changes anyway.

Dr. Seuss tells another story about the Sneetches. The superior race, the ones that everybody aspires to be like and also the ones that everybody hates, are the Star-Belly Sneetches; they have stars on their bellies, and everybody else doesn't. One very clever fellow knew how predictable these Sneetches were, so he came in with a big machine that would put a star on your belly. All the Sneetches *without* a star on their belly rushed in and came out *with* a star on their belly, but of course the original Star-Belly Sneetches still knew who—and how superior—they were. They weren't thrown by this at all. But to facilitate this very predictable situation, the same clever fellow came along with a new machine by which you could go in and get the star taken *off* your belly. So all the Star-

Belly Sneetches went into this machine and came out without stars on their belly; the superior ones were now without stars.

The clever fellow kept these two machines going. Sneetches were running in and out, and the money was piling up, but after awhile all the Sneetches experienced shunyata. They didn't know who was who or what was what or who was a Star-Belly Sneetch and who was a non–Star-Belly Sneetch, so after awhile they just had to look at each other without labels or opinions.

Another slogan says, "Train without bias in all areas. It is crucial always to do this pervasively and wholeheartedly." Train without bias, that's the trick. Train without bias, without the labels. This is supported by the whole tonglen practice and lojong teaching, which encourage us to see bias when it comes up and begin to connect with how painful that is, to feel the prejudice, the resentment, the judgment. It's a powerful, compassionate teaching because it respects our intelligence and our innate good heart. It simply says, "Begin to see what you do, and don't necessarily try to change it; just see it." That's how things begin to change. When we say, "Train without bias," the first step is to meditate on bias when you see it arising. This is the same as "Always meditate on whatever provokes resentment." Then one begins to be able to train meticulously and pervasively in all situations.

Often tonglen is taught exactly as this slogan describes—as a way of training pervasively and meticulously with everyone. You can do this practice in any situation. You start with yourself. You can extend the practice to situations in which compassion spontaneously arises, exchanging yourself for someone you want to help. Then you move on to a slightly more difficult area.

This slogan is saying you should extend this practice to everyone, pervasively, not excluding anyone. Move the practice out to what are commonly called neutrals. These are probably the most frequent relationships that we have. They're people we never get to know and aren't even interested in. They're the ones who sit on the sidewalks and don't have any homes, whom we walk past very fast because it's too painful. They're the other people who are also walking by very quickly. Beginning to do tonglen for the ones we haven't noticed might be a difficult practice, but it could be the most valuable—to begin as you walk through the streets of your life to look at the people that you didn't notice before and become curious about them.

When we encounter life situations that spontaneously evoke compassion, it is not necessary to go through all four stages. It's fine to begin with the third stage, the stage of breathing in the pain in the situation that confronts us and breathing out something that will help. It's fine to breathe in the pain and send out relief or love. There is no need to do the other parts—flashing absolute bodhichitta or working with the black, heavy, and hot and white, light, and cool. These can be skipped in daily life when you do tonglen on the spot.

The key to compassionate action is this: everybody needs someone to be there for them, simply to be there.

A friend was severely burned and disfigured. Later she was able to have plastic surgery to improve her looks, but there was a long time when it was difficult to look at her. This was a time of intense isolation. The nurses would just pop into the room and say cheery things and then get out of there as fast as they could. The doctors would march in and say efficient things and look at her charts, but not at her. All who encountered her kept their distance because the sight of her was too troubling, too disturbing. This was even true of her family and friends. People made their duty calls, but there was some sense of not wanting to relate with the horror of this disfigured person. Finally some hospice people started to come. They would sit there and hold her hand, just be there. They didn't know what to say or what she really needed, but they weren't afraid of her, and she realized that what people really need is for others not to be afraid of them and not to distance themselves from them.

That's what tonglen provides—a support for us

just to be there with another human being and try to communicate. Sometimes there's nothing to be said and nothing to be done. Then the deepest communication of all is just to be there.

The practice goes further. We start with the self, extend out to situations where compassion naturally arises, move out further to this area of neutrals, and then we move to enemies. "Be grateful to every Juan." To be truthful, probably no one in this room feels ready to do tonglen for an enemy. Just the word *enemy* is a problem, a label with a lot of emotion behind it, a lot of anger behind it, and a lot of soft spot behind it. Basically you have to start where you are with your loathing or whatever it is you feel, but with an aspiration to widen the circle of compassion.

I've found in my own history of working with this practice of awakening bodhichitta that the circle of compassion widens at its own speed and widens spontaneously; it's not something you can make happen. It's definitely not something you can fake. But I guess there's a little bit of encouragement to at least experiment with faking it occasionally by seeing what happens when you try to do tonglen for your enemy. There's a lot of encouragement just to try this and see what happens when your enemy is standing in front of you or you're intentionally bringing up the memory of your enemy in order to do tonglen in the meditation hall. Think of this simple instruction: what would it take to be able to communicate with my enemy? What would it take to be able to have my enemy hear what I'm trying to say, and what would it take for me to be able to hear what he or she is trying to say to me? How to communicate from the heart is the essence of what tonglen is about.

You can extend even further to all sentient beings, which involves seeing that this practice is extraordinarily vast. Of course, we could use the notion of "all sentient beings" to distance ourselves from pain, to make the immediate, relative situation more abstract and far away. Someone said to me in all seriousness, "I have a very easy time doing tonglen for all sentient beings, but I have a little trouble doing it for my husband." Doing tonglen for all sentient beings doesn't have to be separate from doing it for yourself and your immediate situation. That's the point that has been made again and again. When you connect with your own suffering, reflect that countless beings at this very moment are feeling exactly what you feel. Their story line is different, but the feeling of pain is the same. When you do the practice both for all sentient beings and for yourself, you begin to realize that self and other are not actually different.

20

The Big Squeeze

I F WE WANT to communicate and we have a strong
aspiration to help others—on the level of social
action, on the level of our family, at work in our community, or we just want to be there for people when
they need us—then sooner or later we're going to experience the big squeeze. Our ideals and the reality
of what's really happening don't match. We feel as if
we're between the fingers of a big giant who is
squeezing us. We find ourselves between a rock and
a hard place.

There is often a discrepancy between our ideals
and what we actually encounter. For instance, with
raising children, we have a lot of good ideas, but
sometimes it's very challenging to put together all
the good ideas with the way our children really are,
there at the breakfast table with food all over themselves. Or with meditation, have you noticed how
difficult it is to actually feel emotions without getting totally swept away by them, or how difficult it
is simply to cultivate friendliness toward yourself
when you're feeling completely miserable or pan-
icked or caught up?

There's a discrepancy between your inspiration and the situation as it presents itself, the immediacy of the situation. It's the rub between those two things—the squeeze between reality and vision—that causes you to grow up, to wake up to be 100 percent decent, alive, and compassionate.

The big squeeze is one of the most productive places on the spiritual path and in particular in this journey of awakening the heart. It's worth talking about because when we find ourselves in that place again and again, usually we want to run away; sometimes we want to give up the whole thing. It's like "burn out": it feels extremely uncomfortable and you can't wiggle out of it. It's like a dog that gets its teeth in your arm and you just can't shake it off. Times of the big squeeze feel like crisis periods. We have the aspiration to wake up and to help and at the same time it doesn't seem to work out on our terms. It feels impossible for us to buy our situation and also impossible to throw it out. Being caught in the big squeeze humbles you, and at the same time, it has great vision. This is the interesting part—it softens you and yet it has a big perspective.

Through meditation practice we learn not to reject, but also not to grasp. This is the same paradox that we are presented with in our lives. It's not so much that you do or don't reject, it's more that sometimes you find that you can't do either or that you do both at the same time.

I was invited to teach in a situation with the Sawang, Trungpa Rinpoche's eldest son, in which it wasn't exactly clear what my status was. Sometimes I was treated as a big deal who should come in through a special door and sit in a special seat. Then I'd think, "Okay, I'm a big deal." I'd start running with that idea and come up with big-deal notions about how things should be, and then I'd get the messages back, "Oh, no, no, no. You should just sit on the floor and mix with everybody and be one of the crowd." Okay. So now the message was that I should just be ordinary, not set myself up or be the teacher. But as soon as I was getting comfortable with being humble, I would be asked to do some special something or other that only big deals did. This was a painful experience because I was always being insulted and humiliated by my own expectations. As soon as I was sure how it should be, so I could feel secure, I would get a message that it should be the other way.

Finally I said to the Sawang, "This is really hurting. I just don't know who I'm supposed to be," and he said, "Well, you have to learn to be big and small at the same time." I think that's the point. We can always get comfortable being either big *or* small, either right *or* wrong.

Although we think that wrong is bad, if we get into the habit of thinking that we are wrong, that can be quite comfortable too. *Any* ground will do; we just want to be able to get our ground, either as a loser or as a winner, as a big deal or an ordinary deal. But if we wish to communicate, if we really wish to open our hearts, sooner or later we are going to find ourselves in the big squeeze, where we can't buy it and we can't throw it out, and we are caught in the juicy situation of being big and small at the same time.

Life is glorious, but life is also wretched. It is both. Appreciating the gloriousness inspires us, encourages us, cheers us up, gives us a bigger perspective, energizes us. We feel connected. But if that's all that's happening, we get arrogant and start to look down on others, and there is a sense of making ourselves a big deal and being really serious about it, wanting it to be like that forever. The gloriousness becomes tinged by craving and addiction.

On the other hand, wretchedness—life's painful aspect—softens us up considerably. Knowing pain is a very important ingredient of being there for another person. When you are feeling a lot of grief, you can look right into somebody's eyes because you feel you haven't got anything to lose—you're just there. The wretchedness humbles us and softens us, but if we were only wretched, we would all just go down the tubes. We'd be so depressed, discouraged, and hopeless that we wouldn't have enough energy to eat an apple. Gloriousness and wretchedness need each other. One inspires us, the other softens us. They go together.

*   *   *

Today's slogans are instructions on how to communicate from the heart. The emphasis is on how to keep one's heart open for the juiciness and richness of the big squeeze. One of the slogans is "Whichever of the two occurs, be patient." Whether it is glorious or wretched, delightful or hateful, be patient. Patience means allowing things to unfold at their own speed rather than jumping in with your habitual response to either pain or pleasure. The real happiness that underlies both gloriousness and wretchedness often gets short-circuited by our jumping too fast into the same habitual pattern.

Patience is not learned in safety. It is not learned when everything is harmonious and going well. When everything is smooth sailing, who needs patience? If you stay in your room with the door locked and the curtains drawn, everything may seem harmonious, but the minute anything doesn't go your way, you blow up. There is no cultivation of patience when your pattern is to just try to seek harmony and smooth everything out. Patience implies willingness to be alive rather than trying to seek harmony.

A hermit well known for his austerity had been practicing in a cave for twenty years. An unconventional teacher named Patrul Rinpoche showed up at the cave, and the hermit humbly and sweetly welcomed him in. Patrul Rinpoche said, "Tell me, what have you been doing here?" "I've been practicing the perfection of patience," the hermit answered.

Putting his face very close to the hermit's face, Patrul Rinpoche said, "But a pair of old scoundrels like us, we don't care anything about patience really. We only do this to get everyone's admiration, right? We just do this to get people to think we are big shots, don't we?" And the hermit started getting irritated. But Patrul Rinpoche wouldn't stop. He just kept laughing and patting him on the back and saying, "Yeah, we sure know how to dupe people, don't we? We really know. I'll bet they bring you a lot of gifts, don't they?" At this point the hermit stood up and screamed, "Why did you come here? Why are you tormenting me? Go away and leave me in peace!" And then the Rinpoche said, "So now, where is your perfection of patience?" So that's the point. We can create the ideal situation in which we have a very high opinion of ourselves, but how do we do when it comes to the big squeeze?

The next slogan is "Don't be swayed by external circumstances." If something is glorious or even just slightly pleasant, you say, "Wow! I want that." If it's wretched or even just slightly irritating, you say, "I want *out* of it!" The point is that challenges don't cease, and if you wish to keep your heart open, the challenges will quickly increase rather than decrease. Harmony may seem a distant hope.

Lest you be hard on yourself about being swayed by external circumstances, keep in mind the story of

Shakyamuni Buddha. Just before the moment of his enlightenment, all of the external circumstances came to try to sway him in the form of the daughters of Mara. (Mara symbolizes the ways we have of looking for alternatives to being where we are.)

Just before he was enlightened, every kind of idea occurred to the Buddha. It was as if every challenge in the book came up. On that evening what was different was that he simply held his seat, opened his heart to whatever might arise, didn't shut down, and was fully there. Lest you feel bad about yourself, not being swayed by external circumstances as a total experience is called enlightenment.

The slogan "Don't vacillate" very much goes along with not being swayed by external circumstances. Whatever arises, you can keep your heart open. Beyond that, you can see shutting down or closing off as an opportunity to wake up. Spinning off when things are painful or pleasant presents an opportunity to practice lojong. You have good instructions on what to do with pain, breathing it in, becoming more intimate and making friends with it; you have instructions on what to do with pleasure, sending it out, giving away what you are most unwilling to lose. In this way we can begin to know the pain of others and wish for others to have happiness, using the joy and pleasure of our lives not as problems but as tools for benefiting others.

* * *

The next slogan is "Don't expect applause," which means "Don't expect thanks." This is important. When you open the door and invite all sentient beings as your guests, and not only that, but you also open the windows, and the walls even start falling down, you find yourself in the universe with no protection at all. Now you're in for it. If you think that just by doing that you are going to feel good about yourself, and you are going to be thanked right and left—no, that won't happen. More than to expect thanks, it would be helpful just to expect the unexpected; then you might be curious and inquisitive about what comes in the door. We can begin to open our hearts to others when we have no hope of getting anything back. We just do it for its own sake.

On the other hand, it's good to express our gratitude to others. It's helpful to express our appreciation of others. But if we do that with the motivation of wanting them to like us, we can remember this slogan. We can thank others, but we should give up all hope of getting thanked back. Simply keep the door open without expectations.

There is also a slogan that says "Don't misinterpret." Don't impose the wrong notion of what harmony is, what compassion is, what patience is, what generosity is. Don't misinterpret what these things really are. There is compassion and there is *idiot* compassion;

there is patience and there is *idiot* patience; there is generosity and there is *idiot* generosity. For example, trying to smooth everything out to avoid confrontation, not to rock the boat, is not what's meant by compassion or patience. It's what is meant by control. Then you are not trying to step into unknown territory, to find yourself more naked with less protection and therefore more in contact with reality. Instead, you use the idiot forms of compassion and so forth just to get ground. When you open the door and invite in all sentient beings as your guests, you have to drop your agenda. Many different people come in. Just when you think you have a little scheme that is going to work, it doesn't work. It was very beneficial to Juan, but when you tried it on Mortimer, he looked at you as if you were crazy, and when you try it on Juanita, she gets insulted.

Coming up with a formula won't work. If you invite all sentient beings as your guests while just wanting harmony, sooner or later you'll find that one of your guests is behaving badly and that just sitting there cheerfully doing your tonglen and trying to cultivate harmony doesn't work.

So you sit there and you say, "Okay, now I'm going to make friends with the fact that I am hurting and afraid, and this is really awful." But you are just trying to avoid conflict here; you just don't want to make things worse. Then all the guests are misbehaving; you work hard all day and they just sit around, smoking cigarettes, drinking beer, eating your food, and then beating you up. You think you're being a warrior and a bodhisattva by doing nothing and saying nothing, but what you're being is a coward. You're just afraid of making the situation worse. Finally they kick you out of your house and you're sitting on the sidewalk. Somebody walks by and says, "What are you doing sitting out here?" You answer, "I am practicing patience and compassion." That's missing the point.

Even though you've dropped your agenda, even though you are trying to work *with* situations instead of struggling *against* them, nevertheless you may have to say, "You can stay here tonight, but tomorrow you're going, and if you don't get out of here, I am calling the police." You don't really know what's going to benefit somebody, but it doesn't benefit anybody to allow someone to beat you up, eat all your food, and put you out on the street.

So "Don't misinterpret" really gets at the notion of the big squeeze. It's saying that you don't know what's going to help, but you need to speak and act with clarity and decisiveness. Clarity and decisiveness come from the willingness to slow down, to listen to and look at what's happening. They come from opening your heart and not running away. Then the action and the speech are in accord with what needs to be done, for you and for the other person.

We make a lot of mistakes. If you ask people whom

you consider to be wise and courageous about their lives, you may find that they have hurt a lot of people and made a lot of mistakes, but that they used those occasions as opportunities to humble themselves and open their hearts. We don't get wise by staying in a room with all the doors and windows closed.

"Train in the three difficulties" is my favorite slogan because it acknowledges that this path is difficult, all right, but it's a good way to spend our time. There are three difficulties. The first is *seeing neurosis as neurosis,* and the second is *being willing to do something different.* The third difficulty is *the aspiration to make this a way of life.*

Seeing neurosis as neurosis. The first difficulty is to see what you do. There is a slogan that goes along with that that says, "Liberate yourself by examining and analyzing." This is an interesting point, to be able to see what we do without hating ourselves. This can also be a description of *maitri*—loving-kindness. We could see what we do with honesty but with gentleness. We could see what we do and realize that that's our first experience of the big squeeze. It's the path of a warrior, seeing what we do without turning it against ourselves.

This slogan about liberating yourself by examining and analyzing simply means, as with the slogans "Don't be jealous," "Don't be frivolous," and "Don't wallow in self-pity," that the first step is to *see* yourself jealous, *see* yourself frivolous, *see* yourself wallowing in self-pity. You think to yourself, "Well, what would Dr. Seuss do in this situation?" Instead of using it as ammunition against yourself, you can lighten up and realize it's the information that you need in order to keep your heart open. If everybody on the planet could experience seeing what they do with gentleness, everything would start to turn around very fast, even if we didn't get to the second difficulty.

Doing something different. The second difficulty is to do something different. Even if you see what you do, can you then do something different? If you're jealous, can you snap your fingers and no longer be jealous? We all know it's more difficult than that. You're sitting there and your boyfriend is sitting across the room with somebody else having a really good time, and you're getting more jealous and furious by the minute. There's a little bird on your shoulder who says, "OK, here's your big chance. You could use this to wake up." And you say, "Forget it! He's really a creep. I want to be mad at him. He deserves my anger." Now the little bird is jumping up and down, saying, "Hey, hey, hey, hey! Don't you remember? Don't you remember?" You're saying, "I don't believe this stuff! I am right to be jealous, and he is horrible!" There you are. The little bird jumps up to the other shoulder and pulls on your earlobe and says, "Come on, come on! Give yourself a break. Get to know this stuff. Drop the story line." "Forget it!" you say. Boy are you stubborn.

That's what I find about myself. Even when we're given the methods for how to give ourselves a break, we are so stubborn. If you think smoking is hard to give up, try giving up your habitual patterns. It leaves you with the same kind of queasy feeling that you have when giving up any other addiction.

So instead of "liberating yourself by examining and analyzing," the habitual response to seeing yourself clearly is to take the wrong medicine: you inflame the jealousy, you wallow more in self-pity, you speed up the frivolity. Usually we do this by talking to ourselves. It's like a bellows fanning a fire. We just sit there, and we have fantasies about our boyfriend leaving the party with our friend, or we talk to ourselves about how it's hopeless and how we always feel like this and how it's never going to get better.

Do something different, such as tonglen. *Anything* different would help, anything that's not habitual. For example, you could go up and take a cold shower and sing at the top of your lungs, or drink a glass of water from the wrong side, like you do when you are trying to get rid of hiccups.

Continuing that way. But even if you see what you do and even if you do something different, the third difficulty is that it's difficult to continue that way, to cut the habitual pattern as a way of life. So whenever you see yourself spinning off in some kind of habitual way, you could aspire to catch yourself and to do something different as a way of cultivating compassion for yourself and compassion for others. But don't be surprised or give up when it's difficult.

A slogan that encourages practicing the three difficulties is "Two activities: one at the beginning, one at the end." At the beginning of your day when you wake up, express your aspiration: "May I practice the three difficulties. May I see what I do. When it happens, may I do something different, and may that be a way of life for me." At the beginning of your day, using your own language, you could encourage yourself to keep your heart open, to remain curious, no matter how difficult things get. Then at the end of the day when you're just about to go to sleep, review the day. Rather than using what happened as ammunition for feeling bad about yourself, about how the whole day went by and you never once remembered what you had aspired to do in the morning, you can simply use it as an opportunity to get to know yourself better and to see all the funny ways in which you trick yourself, all the ways in which you're so good at zoning out and shutting down. If you feel like you don't want to practice the three difficulties anymore because it's like setting yourself up for failure, generate a kind heart toward yourself. Reflecting over just one day's activities can be painful, but you may end up respecting yourself more, because you see that a lot happened; you weren't just one way. As Carl Jung said at the end of his life, "I am astonished, disappointed, pleased with myself. I am distressed, depressed, rapturous. I am all these things at once and cannot add up the sum."

So that's the big squeeze. Although you listen to all these teachings, and you have all these practices as a support, somehow it has to become real for you. It has to be digested by you. The teachings and practices are like orange juice concentrate—that thick orange stuff in the can—and life is like the water. You have to mix it all together. Then you have good orange juice that you can bring out in a big pitcher for everyone to drink. And even though it came out of a can, you know that it's truly freshly squeezed.

2 1

High-Stakes Practice

POGO SAID, "We have met the enemy and they are us." This particular slogan now appears a lot in the environmental movement. It isn't somebody else who's polluting the rivers—it's us. The cause of confusion and bewilderment and pollution and violence isn't really someone else's problem: it's something we can come to know in ourselves. But in order to do that we have to understand that *we have met the friend and that is me*. The more we make friends with ourselves, the more we can see that our ways of shutting down and closing off are rooted in the mistaken thinking that the way to get happy is to blame somebody else.

It's a little uncertain who is "us" and who is "them." Bernard Glassman Sensei, who does a lot of work with the homeless in New York, said that he doesn't work with the homeless because he's such a great guy but because going into the areas of society that he has rejected is the only way to make friends with the parts of himself that he's rejected. It's all interrelated.

We work on ourselves in order to help others, but also we help others in order to work on ourselves. That's a very important point. We could say that working with others is a high-stakes maitri practice, because when we start to work with others, somehow they all seem to end up looking like Juan or Juanita. If we are wholehearted about wanting to be there for other people without shutting anybody or anything out of our hearts, our pretty little self-image of how kind or compassionate we are gets completely blown. We're always being tested and we're always meeting our match. The more you're willing to open your heart, the more challenges come along that make you want to shut it.

You can't do this work in a safety zone. You have to go out into the marketplace and live your life like everybody else, but with the added ingredient of not wanting to shut anything out of your heart. Maitri—loving-kindness—has to go very deep, because when you practice it, you're going to see everything about yourself. Every time your buttons get pushed is like a big mirror showing you your own face, and like the evil stepmother in "Snow White and the Seven Dwarfs," you want the mirror to tell you what you want to hear—even if it's that you haven't been kind or that you're selfish. Somehow you can even use your insight into your limitations to keep yourself feeling all right.

What we don't want is any *unforeseen* feedback from the mirror. What we don't want is to be naked, exposed. We have blind spots, and we put a lot of energy into staying blind. One day the wicked stepmother went to the mirror and said, "Mirror, mirror, on the wall, who's the fairest of them all?" and instead of, "You are, sweetheart," the mirror said, "Snow White." And just like us, she didn't want to hear it. Nevertheless, I think we all know that there's no point in blaming the mirror when it shows you your own face, and there's certainly no point in breaking the mirror.

I once knew a very powerful woman who always managed to have everything go her way. The epitome of her approach to life was that she had a scale in her bathroom that was always turned down so that when she stood on it she weighed exactly what she wanted to weigh. When you look in the mirror and see that you have a big pimple on the end of your nose, and you decide to actually see it and let yourself wince and feel the embarrassment and nevertheless just go about your business, then when a five-year-old comes rushing up to you and says, "Hey lady, you have a big pimple on the end of your nose!" you just say, "I know." But if you try to cover that pimple over with cosmetics or a nosebag, you are shocked and offended when it turns out that everyone can see it anyway.

This tendency to refer back to ourselves, to try to protect ourselves, is so strong and all-pervasive. A simple way of turning it around is to develop our curiosity and our inquisitiveness about everything. This is another way of talking about helping others, but of course the process also helps us. The whole path seems to be about developing curiosity, about looking out and taking an interest in all the details of our lives and in our immediate environment.

When we find ourselves in a situation in which our buttons are being pushed, we can choose to repress or act out, or we can choose to practice. If we can start to do the exchange, breathing in with the intention of keeping our hearts open to the embarrassment or fear or anger that we feel, then to our surprise we find that we're also open to what the other person is feeling. Open heart is open heart. Once it's open, your eyes and your mind are also open, and you can see what's happening in the faces and hearts of other people. If you're walking down the street and way off in the distance—so far away that you can't possibly do anything about it—you see a man beating his dog, and you feel helpless, you can start to do the exchange. You start out doing it for the dog, then you find you're doing it for the man. Then you're also doing it for your own heartbreak and for all the animals and people who are abusing and abused, and for all the people like you who are watching and don't know what to do. Simply by doing this exchange you have made the world a larger, more loving place.

There's a traditional teaching about regarding all sentient beings as your mother. Everyone has been your mother; they've been kind to you and you've had an intimate relationship with them. This teaching always seemed old-fashioned to me. Then I read a book by Joanna Macy in which she recounted being in India and hearing a Tibetan teach on this subject. It was so boring that she went outside to get some air. As she was walking along a path, toward her came an old woman, bent under a load of wood that she was carrying on her back. Suddenly she thought, "This woman was once my mother." Even though she had walked past lots of men and women like this in India, people carrying heavy loads and all bent over so that you couldn't even see their faces, she wanted to see the face of this woman. She wanted to know who this woman was, because all she could think about was how this woman had been her mother.

I learned something from Joanna Macy's story: this teaching that all sentient beings have been our mothers is about taking an interest in other people, about being curious, and about being kind. All those nameless people in the street, they've been your lovers, your brothers and sisters, your fathers and mothers, your children, your friends. Even if you don't buy that, you can just wonder who they are and begin to look at them with some interest and curiosity. Everyone is just like us. We all have our lives; we think that we're the center of the universe, and none of us is paying too much attention to anyone else unless things get very passionate or very aggressive.

*   *   *

Today's slogan is "Take on the three principal causes." The three principal causes are what help us to keep our heart open, to remember to exchange ourselves for others, and to communicate. They are the teacher, the teachings, and a precious human birth.

The teacher. First we'll consider the teacher. In the lojong teachings the teacher is referred to as the spiritual friend, the *kalyanamitra*. The teacher is like a senior warrior, or a student warrior who's further along the path. It's somebody who inspires you to walk the path of warriorship yourself. Looking at them reminds you of your own softness, your own clarity of mind, and your own ability to continually step out and open. Something about them speaks to your heart; you want to have a friendship with this person as a teacher. Trust is an essential ingredient: if you enter into a serious relationship with a teacher, you make a commitment to stick with them and they make a commitment to stick with you, so you're stuck together.

Lest one romanticize this relationship, I'd like to repeat something that Trungpa Rinpoche once said: "The role of the spiritual friend is to insult you." This is true. It isn't that the spiritual friend phones you up and calls you names or sends you letters about what a jerk you are. It's more that the spiritual friend is the ultimate Juan. All your blind spots are going to come out with the spiritual friend. The only difference between the spiritual friend and everybody else in your life is that you've made a commitment to stick with him or her through thick or thin, better or worse, richer or poorer, in sickness and in death. We're not too good at keeping commitments these days; this isn't an age where commitment is honored very widely. If you enter into a relationship with a spiritual friend, you're really asking for it. Rather than the cozy, nurturing situation you might have imagined in the beginning—that the teacher is always kind and will replace the mother or father who never loved you or is finally the friend who has unconditional love for you—you find that in this relationship you begin to see the pimples on your nose, and the mirror on the wall isn't telling you that you're the fairest of them all. To the degree that anything is hidden in this relationship, you begin to see it.

Spending time with Trungpa Rinpoche felt like the great exposé. Often he would say very little. You'd have some seemingly enormous problem. When you finally got to talk with him, it didn't seem so important anymore. Nevertheless, you'd start to crank up the emotion, and he would just sit there and maybe even look out the window or yawn. But even if he sat there just looking and listening, you still felt exposed to yourself. Even if you were with a group and it didn't seem like you were being noticed, you felt all your awkwardness.

With a teacher you feel all the ways in which you

try to con the situation, you feel all the ways in which you try to make yourself look good. You're seeing clearly what you do all the time. But you've made this commitment—one you're not going to run away from, you're not going to write off. This time you're going to stick with it. Staying there becomes like the three difficulties. When you're with the spiritual friend or even thinking about him or her, you begin to see neurosis as neurosis. That encourages you to practice the second difficulty, which is to begin to apply the teachings. And finally, you long to make that a way of life. The spiritual friend does not confirm your existence but serves as a mirror for you to see where you're stuck. The relationship encourages you to wake up.

The most important thing about the relationship with the spiritual friend is that it's basic training for how you relate to every situation in your life. It's all training for you to be grateful to every Juan, and not just the Juan or Juanita that you call your spiritual friend. So when your buttons get pushed, you begin to see that what's happening is your teacher. When your cover has been blown, you begin to see that situation as your teacher. You realize that you know what to do and can begin to relate directly with that pain and use it to relate with the pain of all sentient beings. When you feel inspired and joyful, you can share that with others and develop a sense of kinship.

* * *

The teachings and practices. The second principal cause is the teachings and practices. You have a lot of support when you see what you do rather than turn it against yourself or try to run away from it. You have a lot of encouragement from the teachings and practices to open your heart further, to feel what's going on and not shut down, extending your openness to other sentient beings. When the mirror has just told you that you're not the fairest of them all, and you're feeling embarrassed and awkward, it begins to occur to you that there are many other people at this very moment feeling the same way. You can breathe it in for all of you. When you're feeling happy, it begins to occur to you to think of others and wish for all beings to be happy.

Precious human birth. So the first principal cause is the teacher, who serves as an example and represents life itself, and who also serves as a pointed reminder to let go of holding on to yourself. The second is the teachings and the practices that actually give you tools for opening your heart. And the third cause is this precious human birth. All of us have this precious human birth. We're fortunate enough not to be starving; we're fortunate enough to have food and shelter; we're fortunate enough to hear the teachings and be given methods to wake up; we're fortunate enough to have good intelligence and the luxury to explore and question why we and others suffer.

* * *

Another slogan says, "This time, practice the main points." What that's saying is that for all of us it's a crucial time. We have everything we need to open our hearts, and to work with others in a genuine way. We have a precious human birth; we're not starving in Somalia. We're not living in a country where we grow up being taught to shoot anybody who's on the other side. We have a tremendous amount going for us, so this is the crucial time to practice the main points.

In the slogan "Pay heed that the three never wane," the three are gratitude to your teacher, gratitude to the teachings and the practices, and a commitment to keep the basic vows that you've taken. Gratitude to the teacher starts with making a commitment never to give up on that one person, who has also made a commitment never to give up on you. When I think of my own teacher I feel enormous gratitude continually, practically every moment of my life. It's gratitude that there was somebody who was brave enough and fierce enough and humorous enough and compassionate enough to get it through my thick skull that there's no place to hide. I feel gratitude to the teachings and the practices because they're good medicine and they help us to uncover that soft spot that's been covered over for a very long time.

Finally, we pay heed that the refuge vow and bodhisattva vows never wane. The refuge vow is a commitment not to seek islands of safety any longer but to learn how to leap, how to fly, how to leave the nest and go into uncharted territory, no longer hampered by tiny, self-centered views and opinions. The bodhisattva vow is highstakes practice because it's about giving up privacy and the comfort orientation altogether as a way of awakening your heart further to yourself and to all sentient beings.

In general, we should pay heed that gratitude and appreciation for everything that happens to us never wane. Whether we consider what happens to us good fortune or ill fortune, appreciation for this life can wake us up and give us the courage we need to stay right there with whatever comes through the door.

22

Train Wholeheartedly

NOW IT'S TIME for us to continue our journey and "walk it like we talk it." One of the final slogans is "Observe these two, even at the risk of your life." It refers once again to the refuge and bodhisattva vows. It has a sense of urgency—"even at the risk of your life"—that's telling us not to be afraid to leave the nest. Don't be afraid of losing ground or of things falling apart or of not having it all together.

The meaning of observing the essence of the refuge vow even at the risk of your life is "no escape, no problem." To observe the bodhisattva vow is to exchange ourselves for others and develop compassion for ourselves and others. So even at the risk of our own lives, if it's painful, breathe it in and think about all of the other people who are experiencing pain. If it's delightful, give it away and wish for all people to have that delight. That's the essence of this slogan; it's a revolutionary idea.

Here is one last story about exchanging self for others. I met a young man who had been on a spiritual journey most of his life. He was awake but smug. He suffered from what's called spiritual pride. He was complaining about his girlfriend, who was having

a hard time giving up smoking; the anxiety was triggering an old eating disorder. The young man said he
just kept telling her to be strong, not to be so fearful,
to be disciplined. And she would tell him, "I'm trying.
I'm really trying. I'm doing the best I can." He was
angry because it didn't seem to him that she was trying. He said, "I know I shouldn't be getting so angry
about this. I know I should be more compassionate.
But I just can't help it. It gets under my skin. I want
to be more understanding, but she's so stuck." Then
he heard himself say, "I'm trying. I'm really trying. I'm
doing the best I can." When he heard himself saying
her words, he got the message. He understood what
she was up against, and it humbled him.

I think that all of us are like eagles who have forgotten that we know how to fly. The teachings are
reminding us who we are and what we can do. They
help us notice that we're in a nest with a lot of old
food and old diaries, excrement and stale air. From
when we were very young we've had this longing to
see those mountains in the distance and experience
that big sky and the vast ocean, but somehow we got
trapped in that nest, just because we forgot that we
knew how to fly. We are like eagles, but we have on
underwear and pants and shirt and socks and shoes
and a hat and coat and boots and mittens and a
Walkman and dark glasses, and it occurs to us that
we could experience that vast sky, but we'd better
start taking off some of this stuff. So we take off the

coat and the hat and it's cold, but we know that we have to do it, and we teeter on the edge of the nest and we take off. Then we find out for ourselves that everything has to go. You just can't fly when you are wearing socks and shoes and coats and pants and underwear. Everything has to go.

Marpa the Translator was Milarepa's teacher. He walked all the way from Tibet to India three times in order to get the teachings. Once when he was returning from India, he was with a companion whom he met every so often to compare who was getting the most teachings. His companion became jealous because he felt that Marpa was getting more. When they were in a boat in the middle of a turbulent river, his friend took all of the texts that Marpa had collected and threw them overboard. Talk about an opportunity for tonglen! Marpa didn't exactly feel friendly toward this man. But he realized when he got back to Tibet that he had understood something about all of those teachings in all of those books. He really didn't need it all written down. He had understood something; he had digested something. The teachings and himself had become one.

Each of us has also understood something, and that's what we'll take away from our study and practice of these teachings. These are things that are going to be part of our being now, part of the way that we see things and hear things and smell things.

We try so hard to hang on to the teachings and "get

it," but actually the truth sinks in like rain into very hard earth. The rain is very gentle, and we soften up slowly at our own speed. But when that happens, something has fundamentally changed in us. That hard earth has softened. It doesn't seem to happen by trying to get it or capture it. It happens by letting go; it happens by relaxing your mind, and it happens by the aspiration and the longing to want to communicate with yourself and others. Each of us finds our own way.

The very last slogan is "Train wholeheartedly." You could say, "Live wholeheartedly." Let everything stop your mind and let everything open your heart. And you could say, "Die wholeheartedly, moment after moment." Moment after moment, let yourself die wholeheartedly.

I have a friend who is extremely ill, in the final stages of cancer. The other night Dzongzar Khyentse Rinpoche telephoned her, and the very first words he said were, "Don't even think for a moment that you're not going to die." That's good advice for all of us; it will help us to live and train wholeheartedly.

These teachings are elusive, even though they seem so concrete: if it hurts, breathe in it; if it's pleasant, send it out. It isn't really something that you finally and completely "get." We can read Trungpa Rinpoche's commentaries on mind training and read the text by Jamgön Kongtrül. We can read them and try to apply them to our lives, and we can let them continually haunt us, haunt us into understanding what it really means to exchange oneself for others. What does that really mean? And what does it mean to be a child of illusion? What does it mean to drive all blames into oneself or to be grateful to everyone? What is bodhichitta, anyway? Trying to speak these teachings to you is—for me—a chance to digest them further. Now you are going to find yourself speaking them and living them and digesting them. May you practice these teachings and take them to heart. May you make them your own and spread them to others.

APPENDIX

The Root Text of the Seven Points of Training the Mind

CHEKAWA YESHE DORJE

POINT ONE: *The Preliminaries, Which Are a Basis for Dharma Practice*

I prostrate to the Great Compassionate One.
First, train in the preliminaries.

Point Two: *The Main Practice, Which Is Training in Bodhichitta*

Absolute Bodhichitta
Regard all dharmas as dreams.
Examine the nature of unborn awareness.
Self-liberate even the antidote.
Rest in the nature of alaya, the essence.
In postmeditation, be a child of illusion.

Relative Bodhichitta
Sending and taking should be practiced alternately.

These two should ride the breath.

Three objects, three poisons, and three seeds of virtue.

In all activities, train with slogans.

Begin the sequence of sending and taking with yourself.

POINT THREE: *Transformation of Bad Circumstances into the Path of Enlightenment*

When the world is filled with evil,

Transform all mishaps into the path of bodhi.

Drive all blames into one.

Be grateful to everyone.

Seeing confusion as the four kayas

Is unsurpassable shunyata protection.

Four practices are the best of methods.

Whatever you meet unexpectedly, join with meditation.

POINT FOUR: *Showing the Utilization of Practice in One's Whole Life*

Practice the five strengths,

The condensed heart instructions.

The mahayana instruction for ejection of consciousness at death

Is the five strengths: how you conduct yourself
  is important.

Point Five: *Evaluation of Mind Training*

All dharma agrees at one point.

Of the two witnesses, hold the principal one.

Always maintain only a joyful mind.

If you can practice even when distracted, you are
  well trained.

Point Six: *Disciplines of Mind Training*

Always abide by the three basic principles.

Change your attitude, but remain natural.

Don't talk about injured limbs.

Don't ponder others.

Work with the greatest defilements first.

Abandon any hope of fruition.

Abandon poisonous food.

Don't be so predictable.

Don't malign others.

Don't wait in ambush.

Don't bring things to a painful point.

Don't transfer the ox's load to the cow.

Don't try to be the fastest.

Don't act with a twist.

Don't make gods into demons.

Don't seek others' pain as the limbs of your own happiness.

POINT SEVEN: *Guidelines of Mind Training*

All activities should be done with one intention.

Correct all wrongs with one intention.

Two activities: one at the beginning, one at the end.

Whichever of the two occurs, be patient.

Observe these two, even at the risk of your life.

Train in the three difficulties.

Take on the three principal causes.

Pay heed that the three never wane.

Keep the three inseparable.

Train without bias in all areas. It is crucial always to do this pervasively and wholeheartedly.

Always meditate on whatever provokes resentment.

Don't be swayed by external circumstances.

This time, practice the main points.

Don't misinterpret.

Don't vacillate.

Train wholeheartedly.

Liberate yourself by examining and analyzing.

Don't wallow in self-pity.

Don't be jealous.

Don't be frivolous.

Don't expect applause.

When the five dark ages occur,

This is the way to transform them into the path
   of bodhi.

This is the essence of the *amrita* of the oral
   instructions,

Which were handed down from the tradition of
   the sage of Suvarnadvipa.

Having awakened the karma of previous training

And being urged on by intense dedication,

I disregarded misfortune and slander

And received oral instruction on taming ego-
   fixation.

Now, even at death, I will have no regrets.

BIBLIOGRAPHY

Chödrön, Pema. *The Wisdom of No Escape and the Path of Loving-Kindness.* Boston and London: Shambhala Publications, 1991.

Kongtrül, Jamgön. *The Great Path of Awakening.* Translated by Ken McLeod. Boston and London: Shambhala Publications, 1987.

Trungpa, Chögyam. *Cutting Through Spiritual Materialism.* Edited by John Baker and Marvin Casper. Boston and London: Shambhala Publications, 1973.

————. *The Heart of the Buddha.* Edited by Judith L. Lief. Boston and London: Shambhala Publications, 1991.

————. *The Myth of Freedom and the Way of Meditation.* Edited by John Baker and Marvin Casper. Boston and London: Shambhala Publications, 1976.

————. *Shambhala: The Sacred Path of the Warrior.* Edited by Carolyn Rose Gimian. Boston and London: Shambhala Publications, 1984.

————. *Training the Mind and Cultivating Loving-Kindness.* Edited by Judith L. Lief. Boston and London: Shambhala Publications, 1993.

RESOURCES

Further teachings from Pema Chödrön on lojong practice are available in *The Compassion Box: Book, CD, and Card Deck* (ISBN 1-59030-075-0). The boxed set features 59 two-color cards with a lojong slogan on one side and original commentary by Pema on the other. Also included are: instructions on how to use the cards; a fold-out stand; a 45-minute audio CD of Pema offering in-depth instructions on tonglen meditation; and a copy of *Start Where You Are*. For more information or to order, visit www.shambhala.com.

For information regarding meditation instruction or inquiries about a practice center near you, please contact one of the following:

Shambhala International
1084 Tower Road, Halifax, NS, Canada B3H 2Y5
phone: (902) 425-4275, ext. 26 • fax: (902) 423-2750
Web site: www.shambhala.org
This Web site contains information about the more than one hundred centers affiliated with Shambhala.

Shambhala Europe
Annostrasse 27-33, D50678 Köln, Germany
phone: 49 221 31024-10 • fax: 49 221 31024-50
Web site: www.shambhala-europe.org

Karmê Chöling
369 Patneaude Lane, Barnet, VT 05821
phone: (802) 633-2384 • fax: (802) 633-3012
Web site: www.karmecholing.org

Shambhala Mountain Center
4921 County Road 68c, Red Feather Lakes, CO 80545
phone: (970) 881-2184 • fax: (970) 881-2909
Web site: www.shambhalamountain.org

Gampo Abbey
Pleasant Bay, NS, Canada B0E 2P0
phone: (902) 224-2752 • fax: (902) 224-1521
Web site: www.gampoabbey.org

Naropa University is the only accredited, Buddhist-inspired university in North America. For more information, contact:

Naropa University
2130 Arapahoe Avenue, Boulder, CO 80302
phone: (303) 444-0202 • fax: (303) 444-0410
e-mail: info@naropa.edu
Web site: www.naropa.edu

Audio- and videotape recordings of talks and seminars by Pema Chödrön are available from:

Great Path Tapes and Books
330 E. Van Hoesen Boulevard, Portage, MI 49002
phone: (616) 384-4167 • fax: (425) 940-8456
e-mail: gptapes@aol.com
Web site: www.pemachodrontapes.org

Kalapa Recordings
1084 Tower Road, Halifax, NS, Canada B3H 2Y5
phone: (902) 420-1118, ext. 19 • fax: (902) 423-2750
e-mail: recordings@shambhala.org
Web site: www.shambhala.org/recordings

Sounds True
P. O. Box 8010, Boulder, CO 80306
phone: (800) 333-9185
Web site: www.soundstrue.com

Cards printed with each of the mind-training slogans, as well as a poster for use in one's practice, are available from:

Vajradhatu Publications
1678 Barrington, Halifax, NS, Canada B3J 2A2
phone: (902) 421-1550
Web site: www.shambhalashop.com

Samadhi Store
30 Church Street, Barnet, VT 05821
phone: (800) 331-7751
Web site: www.samadhicushions.com

Ziji
9148 Kerry Road, Boulder, CO 80303
phone: (800) 565-8470
Web site: www.ziji.com

The *Shambhala Sun* is a bimonthly Buddhist magazine founded by Chögyam Trungpa Rinpoche. For a subscription or sample copy, contact:

Shambhala Sun
P. O. Box 3377, Champlain, NY 12919-9871
phone (toll free): (877) 786-1950
Web site: www.shambhalasun.com

INDEX OF SLOGANS

SHAMBHALA LIBRARY

The Sabbath: Its Meaning for Modern Man,
by Abraham Joshua Heschel.

Shambhala: The Sacred Path of the Warrior, by
Chögyam Trungpa. Edited by Carolyn Rose Gimian.

Siddhartha: A New Translation, by Hermann Hesse.
Translated by Sherab Chödzin Kohn.

Start Where You Are: A Guide to Compassionate Living,
by Pema Chödrön.

Tao Teh Ching, by Lao Tzu. Translated by
John C. H. Wu.

Teachings of the Buddha, edited by Jack Kornfield.

*The Tibetan Book of the Dead: The Great Liberation
through Hearing in the Bardo*, translated with
commentary by Francesca Fremantle and
Chögyam Trungpa.

Training the Mind and Cultivating Loving-Kindness,
by Chögyam Trungpa.

The Way of Chuang Tzu, by Thomas Merton.

*When Things Fall Apart: Heart Advice for Difficult
Times*, by Pema Chödrön.

*The Wisdom of the Desert: Sayings from the Desert
Fathers of the Fourth Century*, by Thomas Merton.

Zen Mind, Beginner's Mind, by Shunryu Suzuki.